I0882868

THE VALUE(S) OF LITERATURE

SUNY Series in Aesthetics and the Philosophy of Art

Mary C. Rawlinson, editor

THE VALUE(S) OF LITERATURE

James S. Hans

State University of New York Press

Published by
State University of New York Press, Albany

© 1990 State University of New York

All rights reserved

Printed in the United States of America

No part of this book may be used or reproduced
in any manner whatsoever without written permission
except in the case of brief quotations embodied in
critical articles and reviews.

For information, address State University of New York
Press, State University Plaza, Albany, N.Y., 12246

Library of Congress Cataloging-in-Publication Data

Hans, James S., 1950–
The value(s) of literature / James S. Hans. p. cm. — (SUNY series in aesthetics and the philosophy of art)
ISBN 0-7914-0205-3. — ISBN 0-7914-0206-1 (pbk.)
1. Literature—Philosophy. 2. Literature—Aesthetics. 3. Poetry—History and criticism. 4. Values in literature. 5. Social values in literature. I. Title. II. Title: Values of literature.
III. Series.
PN49.H34 1990
801′ .3—dc20 89-31513

10 9 8 7 6 5 4 3 2 1

For Heather

CONTENTS

PREFACE

Although *The Value(s) of Literature* clearly and carefully establishes its situation in both the introductory chapter and in the discussion of the poets that follows, I should briefly like to emphasize my intentions in writing this book. As the title suggests, my chief concern is to consider the values in and the value of that which we have traditionally called literature. In doing so, however, I establish a framework that takes issue with three of the most prominent ways of conducting literary studies. In contrast to some of the more traditional modes of criticism that grew out of Modernism, I argue that literature does indeed have everything to do with the values that we put in play every day in the world and that therefore the ethical aspects of literature must be confronted if we are to sustain the work of our writers. In contrast to certain post-structuralistic modes of thought, I suggest that there is indeed value in the word "literature" itself, that even if there is nothing intrinsic to the language we find in a poem or novel that is distinctly "literary," and even if literary forms are not discrete and autotelic structures, that which we call literature is still something we deliberately choose to value in a different way from the kinds of writing we find in other domains like newspapers and commonplace books, and we ought to continue to do so. And in contrast to the political critics of various stripes who have done a great deal to convince us that texts are loci of ethical concerns, I have sought to argue that even as all literature is fundamentally ethical in nature, it is still for the most part deliberately not immediately practical and didactic. In a very real sense there is no road through to action in literature, but that does not mean that poems, novels and other literary genres don't present ethical frameworks with which we need to be concerned if we are going to do justice to the texts we choose to discuss.

The main work of this book, then, is devoted to establishing the kinds of things that need to be said about the ethical context that is inherent in every aesthetic form. In order to speak meaningfully about this question I have chosen to examine a relatively few major poems by Walt Whitman, Wallace Stevens and A. R. Ammons. At the same time,

I have deliberately chosen *not* to involve myself in exhaustive discussions about any of the poets, nor have I devoted space in the text to the ongoing critical appraisal of these poets by other critics. Though I would hope that my remarks about the poets would contribute to the assessment of their work, my primary goal is to determine what should and should not be said about the ethical elements of poetry and other forms of literature. Given this orientation, I have also for the most part eschewed traditional kinds of analysis.

The formal structures of the poems, for example, are not given much attention here, and there are few remarks about the kinds of literary devices the poets employ or the stylistic features that contribute to a new sense of what poetry as a genre is capable of performing. These—and other—kinds of analysis are left out not because I believe they have no place in the discussion of literature—on the contrary, I think that they play an important role in allowing us to discern both the aesthetic nature of the text and the ethic that is implicit in it—but simply so that the points I am trying to make will not be lost in arguments about the value of this or that device, this or that form. If I am not a pluralist in the usual sense of the term—I certainly *don't* think that all modes of analysis are equally valuable any more than I feel that we ought to embrace every way of dealing with texts that presents itself—I do believe that there are a good number of formal and thematic tools that one can and should make use of in the analysis of literature.

I do not provide any specific "new tools" here simply because I don't see the need for yet another methodological grid through which the play of a poem should be filtered. At the same time, it could be said that my refusal to separate the worlds of poetry and everyday life constitutes a methodological choice that entails its own fairly elaborate series of inclusions and exclusions, and I would wholly agree with that. I would hope, however, that the particular choices I make in my discussion of the poetry are seen as less important than the kinds of questions I raise about what ethical problems are germane to literary texts in general. If my remarks contribute to a view of literature that allows us to celebrate its aesthetic richness at the same time that we come to appreciate the kinds of values it seeks to engender, then I shall consider *The Value(s) of Literature* to have accomplished its task.

ACKNOWLEDGMENTS

I have been most fortunate over the years in the friends and colleagues who have come my way, so much so that my acknowledgments are for the most part repetitions of the ones to be found in my earlier books. Allen Mandelbaum, Herbert Lindenberger, Ronald Sharp, and Michael McCanles have generously given of their time and supported my work when I most needed what they so willingly offered. Robert Hedin, Gillian Overing, Dillon Johnston, and Myrddin Jones have provided the kind of local environment that enriches one's life at the same time that they have contributed to my sense of the literary and critical landscape. Carola Sautter has been the ideal editor—interested, supportive, expeditious and pragmatic—and I thank her for her assistance in all the little (and big) ways that make one feel good about the production of one's work. I am also grateful to Wake Forest University for providing the leave that helped me complete work on the manuscript.

As always, my final acknowledgments are to my wife Hilma and my daughter Heather, to whom this book is dedicated. If, as I believe, there is a dialectical relationship between the values of literature and the values of life, then Hilma and Heather are the most important part of this dialectic in my life and therefore have everything to do with the values that are expressed in the following pages. And inasmuch as Heather has been an essential aspect of the ethical fabric of my daily life, I can only hope that some day she will be able to see her contribution to this book, just as I hope that *The Value(s) of Literature* will give something back to her.

INTRODUCTION: THE VALUE(S) OF LITERATURE

During the past twenty years or so we have seen a serious critique of the aesthetic values of the Romantic and Modern poets, and in the process we have learned how to be suspicious of those premises we tend to take for granted. We have learned to be more "critical" in an important way, and this was clearly a salutary development. At the same time, however, one must at some point begin to wonder whether we have become too critical, whether we have lost sight of the literature that was originally our chief concern. One is reminded of Arnold's commentary on his own age, his insistence on the need for a combination of the critical and the creative, and even if we have learned that the distinction between critical and creative is not as easy to draw as Arnold thought, perhaps it is time to question the manner in which our critical disciplines have developed. It has been said that critics are "word people," and this is certainly true. The question is whether the word people have allowed their words to overrun everything, have been blinded by their own commitments to language and have thus lost sight of larger issues.

We know, for example, that in many ways the New Criticism was driven by the force of a new kind of poetry rather than the other way around, and while it is possible for criticism to contribute to the development of poetry as well, it seems that we have been so taken by our own linguistic creations that we have forgotten the poetry that they were supposed to address. In saying so, I recognize that the concept of literature itself has been called into question, but most critics still tacitly acknowledge that there is something more important going on in a poem than in a fashion magazine. Those who would argue otherwise are doing sociology rather than literary criticism, and even if there is a place for this work, it should not supplant the serious discussion of those strange artifacts we call literature.

If we accept that the critiques of language are valuable—and they are—and if we agree that our nostalgia for origins is a real problem, we must still inevitably confront the choice that so many critics seek to avoid; we face the choice of choice. It is (almost) possible in a post-structuralist critique to avoid choosing, to remain playfully between the ironies one's discourse has articulated, but in the end we still choose, after our critique if not within it. And if it is healthy to remain suspicious of any text that suggests there is something "outside of the text," we all know there is an outside of the text every night when we sit down for dinner. We have devalorized the book and valorized language in the process, and this has prevented us from considering the larger parameters of any text. Put another way, we have generated an incredibly rarefied discourse that wilts upon immediate contact with the everyday world, and while many find this preferable, many others do not, poets included. Even when we acknowledge that a poem is nothing more than signs, we must still ask what we are to make of those signs once we are done demystifying them, and this is something we have become unwilling to do.

At the same time, many of our poets and novelists have continued to write about things outside of the text. We have chosen to ignore this, or to locate the nostalgia inherent in their visions of the outside of the text, or we have simply demoted such figures precisely because they are naive enough to assume that there is an outside of the text. A good number of our current novelists and poets, for example, have quite clear commitments to the concerns that developed out of the environmental movement, and yet it is hard to find serious discussions of these concerns in academic journals. We confine ourselves to their words, not to the implications of them, and we have come to think that there is no place in "serious scholarship" to evaluate these "outside" concerns. Our business is with words, nothing more, nothing less, or so it all too often seems.

Inasmuch as I share the environmental concerns of many of our writers, I have regularly been struck by the ways in which our criticism consciously seeks to avoid such questions. Outside of the more commercial products—one thinks of the essays of a writer like Wendell Berry—there is no place for the poet's *values* to be discussed. In the academic world, the closest one comes to an outside of the text is the criticism that abounds, and while there is much that is of value in this work—and much that would connect it to environmental concerns—it is more interested in ideological battles than it is in anything that could be said to be "outside of ideology." In beginning with the social world, it begins too late, for it has already cut off our intrinsic connection to the world that is non-ideological, the world of dirt, water, animals and the like. To be sure, this world of dirt is symbolized by those whose ideologies dominate our signs, and there is no conception of dirt that is non-ideological—we can only construe dirt through signs. But our social critics take this to mean that the question of dirt, therefore, is simply a question of who has power over it, whereas the environmental movement would argue that it is precisely that absurdly human notion of our having power over it in the first place that is so flawed. This is an issue with which the Marxists and feminists remain largely unconcerned, so it drops out of our discourse altogether.

The question with which I am concerned, however, has more to do with the values of our writers than with the environmental movement per se. We have created a discourse that presumes they have, at best, two values: words, and in some cases, social ideology. Writers love words, love to play with words, and sometimes they connect their word play to the ideological implications of language. Beyond that, our discourse would suggest, there is nothing to be said. There are several ways of accounting for this fact, I suppose. One could argue that our tendency toward specialization has prevented us from having sufficient knowledge to comment on anything outside of the text. Our revised conception that there is no outside of the text would prompt us to believe that there is no dirt, only the sign "dirt." Such concerns are in their own way dirty, and we prefer to remain as clean and "objective" in our discourse as we can be. I would argue, however, that for the most part the reason such "outside" matters never get space in academic journals has more to do with the ironic tendencies of twentieth-century writing: we have simply grown accustomed to the comforts of an ironic position. We have come to like the idea that the irony of discourse allows us the illusion of not having to choose, of being able forever to reside in the "deadly space between." Irony is *safe.* It allows us to display our intellectual dexterity without having to commit ourselves to anything. It is also, as Ceslaw Miloz has said, the "glory of slaves,"[1] but we are content with our slavery and see no reason to question it. After all, we may be the slaves of irony, but at least we don't have to make serious choices.

I have long agreed with those who argue that criticism is as "creative" as other forms of writing, that the distinction that makes it secondary and "parasitic" is an artificial one. I have also enjoyed and profited from the great theoretical debates of the past decades. But at the end of the day, when I compare what our critical and theoretical discourse has said in the past twenty years with what our poets and novelists have done, I conclude that we have several fine poets and novelists who not only write, and write well, but write *courageously.* I have a much harder time finding critics and theoreticians who write courageously—for the most part they remain the slaves of irony and content themselves with the "courage" of inaugurating yet another academic revolution in thinking.

The word "courage" itself, though, seems strikingly out of place in the context of literary criticism. What, after all, does courage have to do with academic writing? Scholars and critics don't talk about such things, and any text that does by definition doesn't deserve a place in the respected journals. There are always literary and scholarly skirmishes to be dealt with, and the local and general political battles over the hearts and minds of future writers and scholars, and that's more than enough to deal with. "Courage" is a mushy word, an anachronism, out of place in our sleek modern machine. But if this is so, how are we to deal with the courage of our poets and novelists? Is it appropriate for us to reduce their courage to concerns about language? Is it sufficient to discuss their technical innovations in verse structure and the play of signs in their poems? Is it inevitable that for a writer to be canonized he must be denuded of all value, stripped of any concerns but literary ones?

One of the striking facts of the academic discourse about writing is that it has increasingly moved against the grain of much of the work it deals with. To be sure, all too many twentieth-century texts are preoccupied by the limits of language, and all too many novels and poems are as reflexive and ironic as the critics who discuss them, but there is another strain too, and it tends to get lost in the words. Whitman declared some time ago that he was the poet of the *body* as well as the soul; Williams followed in his path, and many writers of the current generation have written about bodies. Poetry and fiction have increasingly come to articulate a thoroughly *embodied* world, one localized by our brute, physical presence on the planet, equally localized by place and time, yet it would be difficult to see the importance of this tendency in the academic criticism about such writers, even when it emphasizes the ways in which Whitman or Williams wrote of and out of their bodies. Even the most cerebral of our recent poets, Wallace Stevens, said—perhaps all too sadly—"The greatest poverty is not to live in a physical world."[2] Well, what happened to the physical world of which these poets wrote? It has become ironized, "problematized," written out of existence. Poets and critics remain bodily creatures, but it would be hard to tell that from the words of the critics.

A critic's business is words. Yes, but what happens when those words refer to a body? What if those words say "The greatest poverty is not to live in a physical world"? Is a body just another sign and nothing more? Is it no more than a contrasting element in a poem? And what about the other things to which poets refer now and then, things like pain, and joy? Are these too just words, just more signifiers? In a way, yes. And in part we have moved away from talking about such things in our serious journals because there is no way to control discussion about "feelings" or "emotions." We had more than enough such criticism in the earlier part of the century to convince us of that. So pain disappears, joy becomes a signifier, and the poet plays with his words.

The conception of a physical world is indeed a problematic one; pain is problematic too, no less than joy. Sexual activity is trickier still. Such words mean both more and less than they say, and we must be careful when we employ them, lest they quickly reify into mere conventions. But a writer like Stevens is aware of these problems. He is consummately aware of them. No one was more bedeviled and intrigued by the illusions of language, and no Modern poet has been more studiously reflexive than Stevens. Yet on occasion he was still given to saying "The greatest poverty is not to live in a physical world." Is such a line a sad commentary on his own life, cerebral as it was? Is it a reflection of a disguised nostalgia for origins? Is it an ironic articulation of the fact that "it is a world of words to the end of it"?[3] Could it be all of these things and still be a courageous statement of value on Stevens' part? Could it articulate one of the two or three things he learned about the world in his long life? And if so, how are we as critics to deal with his utterance? The worst that can be said of us is that we haven't even bothered to ask these questions. We are word people. Such questions belong in someone else's domain.

There are good historical reasons for our reticence about anything other than words, for our century has tried virtually everything at least once. Psychology, sociology, anthropology, philosophy, history, biology—it seems as though every discipline has been applied to literary texts, and every one has led to one excess or another. So we have retreated. We have narrowed our discourse for the most part to signs as they play off of one another, and signs as the constituent elements of semiotic systems. These are compelling discourses, but there is more to literary texts than what they have to offer, and we have willingly abandoned everything else.

The paralysis of irony is omnipresent, as is all too natural inasmuch as our major theories have depended on it for fifty years. New Criticism, even when it emphasized the ontological level of the poem—as it did in John Crowe Ransom's work—was based on poetry as an ironic structure, on the tensions between statements within a work that could not be resolved. A legitimate proposition in its own way, this ironic principal nevertheless all too often became a way of avoiding talking about anything but irony, and we habituated ourselves to a critical practice that emphasized ironic structure at the expense of everything else in a poem. To be sure, this method works extremely well, particularly when it is applied to Modern poems, whose very essence seems to be the anguish of irony. Eliot's work is nothing if not ironic, and the same could be said for the other major poets and novelists of the period as well. The crucial question, though, is whether this work is *only* ironic, and we haven't yet addressed that issue.

The post-structuralists told us in turn that we weren't really ironists after all, that we were simply using the ironic mode to cover up our desires for a ground to language. Our criticism may have *seemed* ironic, but it was designed to affirm the ontology that was inherent in the play of irony within the poem. We were simply hiding our commitment to ontology under the guise of ambiguity, when in fact we were arguing that *something* existed in between the ironic play. Essence became aporia, and irony took on even more importance. The genius of the post-structuralist argument is that it confronts us with our own contradiction and makes us feel guilty about it. Like T. S. Eliot, we were used to seeing the world as a heap of broken images, but we also secretly desired the unity we imagined former epochs as having. The world was too far gone by the twentieth century to imagine seriously a unified world picture, so we couldn't go that far. Instead, we hypothesized a hidden unity, one locked within the intangible space of irony. And since it seems to be a human characteristic to desire some ground or unity, we couldn't help but feel guilty when the post-structuralists accused us of harboring such secret desires.

And we *were* guilty. The only question is whether or not those desires are entirely unfounded, which is the same question as whether or not a poem is anything more than an ironic structure. In the end, the post-structuralists simply took the already-existing ironic tendencies and turned them into a high art—the dance over the aporia that confirmed one's derring do. This is little more than a blend of feeble existential heroism and deft linguistic play, and even if the best practitioners of this art manage to bring it off, we are still left in the end with the same facile commitment to the power of language and the same confusion about what is outside of the text. The outside of the text has simply been infinitely deferred, placed in some nether world beyond academic concerns altogether. A post-structuralist might well be willing to agree that there is an outside of the text, but if there is, he doesn't have any particular interest in it because he is too busy devoting himself to showing us the ways in which we are trapped by our desire for presence.

In our critical practice, then, there is a stunning lack of concern for anything a poet or novelist might be saying beyond, in addition to, or through the ironic structures that constitute his artifact. If there is an aesthetic, it must necessarily be an aesthetic devoted totally to the artificiality of linguistic structures, or so we seem to think. In a metaphorical way, we have simply continued to play out the dominant strain of Western civilization when we play at being post-structuralist ironists. We have not escaped the tendencies we seek to put out of play—we have simply embraced them more fully. The most pertinent distinction here is the one Milan Kundera makes use of in his novel *The Unbearable Lightness of Being.* Post-structuralism is fully committed to lightness—it maintains that it doesn't want to valorize one side of an ironic structure over another, but underlying its practice is a full commitment to *lightness.* What, after all, would a world devoid of ground be based on if not lightness? What but lightness is the defining characteristic of a world of words alone? We have always preferred lightness of being over heaviness, even if we remain caught in our desire for a ground. The post-structuralists have simply emphasized what Kundera stresses in his title, that in many ways our desire for lightness is unbearable to us. Of course even here there is a comfortable irony, for "to bear" implies weight, which suggests that the lightness of being is finally too heavy for us to hold up, but then one can also look at the title in a different way, one that implies that weightiness is impossible to avoid, however much we pursue lightness. One could even say that it is the play between heaviness and lightness that gives life value.

Weight is what we have left out of the equation in our ironic commitment to words. Heaviness is what we have been avoiding, the heaviness of being. But that heaviness cannot be eliminated simply by placing the word "Being" in quotation marks, for even if the word itself is in question, heaviness is unquestionable, and perhaps more than anything it is the heaviness to which the word "Being" itself refers. We have grown accustomed to thinking of the essence of being in terms of lightness, but that may well have been our biggest mistake. Being is not an airy nothing, a transcendent essence, but rather a specific density, a coherent kind of heaviness that roots us to the ground. Things have *mass* as well as force and movement, and if we cannot separate the mass from movement and force, neither can we separate the force and movement from the mass. And it is this heaviness of being that we have sought to avoid even as our poets and novelists have pointed continually to that weight. We have found no value in weight, in heaviness, so we have assumed that our writers have denied its value as well, even though that is precisely what so many of them affirm.

If we have avoided the heaviness of being, we have in turn read everything in terms of lightness, including our most important writers. Most recent critical theories, for example, trace their origins in one way or another to Nietzsche. He is the tutelary figure of our skepticism just as he seems to express our commitment to irony. But while Nietzsche might serve those purposes very well, there are other aspects to his work that we have sought to ignore or avoid, and I would argue that these are the most important aspects of his writing. The critique of Western values that Nietzsche symbolically inaugurates is something we have become adept at, but in becoming masters of this critique, we avoided the more difficult part of Nietzsche's project, so much so that we have forgotten that there was anything else to his work. Yet over and over again, we find Nietzsche arguing for more than just a critique, as, for example, in this statement from *The Gay Science: "In what do you believe?*—In this, that the weights of all things must be determined anew."[4] Nietzsche's critique of Western values was designed to allow us to weigh anew the things of the world, and yet the result of his work is that we have continually deferred the weighing itself—we simply extended the critique into an all-encompassing game.

But what does it mean that we need to weigh things anew? The most obvious sense of these words is simply that things need to be valued in a new way. The older values no longer apply to the world in which we live, so in order to arrive at a proper sense of things, we need to determine the ways in which the weights of things have changed. But Nietzsche doesn't use the word "value," even if that is what is implied by his statement; rather, he uses the word "weigh," suggesting that valuing itself is based on weighing things. "Weigh" first and foremost refers to a process that involves assessing the mass of objects, just as "thing" suggests something physical and tangible, and while Nietzsche doubtless had other things in mind as well, it is no accident that he chooses these terms from the physical world. To weigh is to value, to assess the mass an object contains, regardless of whether that mass is metaphorically or literally conceived.

But if one begins in the physical world, one seems to be left with an all too pointless task, for if our measuring devices have grown more sophisticated, it remains the case that the weights of the things of this world cannot have changed very much. The measuring devices that have been called into question by the Nietzschean view are metaphysical devices, yet Nietzsche uses a physical conception when he speaks of that which needs to be done. Of course it is precisely because the metaphysical measures have been found faulty that Nietzsche begins again with the physical world. His philosophy is, after all, based on learning to accept the physical world of which we are a part—and coming to accept the physical beings we are as well—so it makes sense for him to use the more prosaic word "weigh." Even more, the larger parameters of his vision suggest that humans do nothing more—or less—than spend their lives continually weighing things anew. Without the metaphysical world and its idealist solace, we must both weigh the things of the world *and* be aware of the fact that the process never ends—our measurements are never precise enough, and the things of the world change too rapidly for us ever to be content with previous measurements.

The important issue here is the relationship between the critique of Western metaphysics and the need to weigh things anew. Is a critique necessarily a weighing in and of itself? That would seem to be the answer most readily proffered these days, for then one could argue that one is indeed weighing things anew by demonstrating the false values of the older system of measurement. This is indeed what our critique is all about. But we are forced back once again to the question of the "outside of the text": texts themselves might have weight, but the things outside of the text more obviously have weight, and we have yet to get around to such things. Nietzsche himself repeatedly emphasized that he saw the critique of Western values as a prelude to the newer measurements of things he hoped to institute, though he also realized that the critique in its own way was part of the renewal of measurement. Was he wrong in thinking there was more to revaluing than endless critique?

The easiest way to argue this point of view would be to discuss the implications of the word "thing" in the quotation above. The word itself is suspect, harboring as it does within it the fact that we determine the values of things by noticing them as things to begin with. And in the twentieth-century world, things have in a real way ceased to exist in two crucial domains. In the critical world, things have disappeared into "signs," never—so far—to be seen again. Things in this realm have become merely reflections of the ideology that notices them in the first place—any system recognizes the existence of this or that thing only to the extent that it can put it to use. So the word "thing" has become suspect at best, and at worst simply outside of the text.

In the domain of physics, things are somewhat different, but here too there has been a striking change. "Things" have again ceased to exist for all practical purposes. We are left with probabilities, force fields, energy quotients and the like, and things—to the extent that they exist in this world—are simply greater concentrations of force or energy than the area surrounding them. In this way things have been exploded, removed from their discrete space and brought into a far larger system of processes and fields. I doubt that Nietzsche would be the least bit distressed by this change, for it fits in quite well with his own desire to weigh things anew. That is, in the end, all that modern physics is doing. Equally important, modern physics has not eliminated the thing; it has simply redefined it in important ways, ways that are again congruent with Nietzsche's own thinking. Just as "things" were gradually reifying into "objects," both Nietzsche and modern science came along to correct our vision. Both told us that there is nothing discrete in the world, that things don't exist apart from other things at all but are instead constantly affected by everything around them. It is important to remember that even as modern physics moved into the world of probabilities and force fields, it did so only by emphasizing different aspects of older "laws." The formula that says "force equals mass times acceleration" came to emphasize force and acceleration more because of the difficulty of measuring the things that were under investigation, but mass didn't disappear when this shift occurred. Likewise, Einstein's famous $E = mc^2$ clearly has mass at its center. It has been de-emphasized in a way, but it is still there, still noticeable, and still crucial to any equation or measurement.

If we in turn make use of the changes in both the critical and the scientific views of a "thing," we can profit in ways we can't if we restrict ourselves to the critical. It is true that "thing" turned into reified object, and we need as a consequence to be critical of the things that were named in the older system of values. But it is equally true that things still exist for all that. They exist within fields and have lost their presumed autonomy, but they do have greater mass within their fields than other areas, and they need to be recognized therefore as measurable, *weighable* quantities. This seems to me to be the entire point of Nietzsche's critique *and* his desire to weigh things anew.

The word "thing" has been newly measured, and the sense of it has changed as a result. In turn the things of the world need to be newly weighed, though this is a process that we have yet sufficiently to begin. Again, it is not difficult to see why we have yet to get around to the second, more difficult part of Nietzsche's project—we need only look at the equivalent of "thing" in the literary world, a "text." More precisely, I suppose, a "book" was a text that became reified over the years until it was seen to occupy its own autonomous space. When the world of texts appears, books are supplanted, for we have come to see that no work exists discretely. This is a salutary revision of our conception of things, but only to the extent that it does not wash itself into absurdity. Texts, like things, might not be the autonomous loci we once thought they were, but they do exist. They may in part have been created to turn literature into a commodity; they may have been localized for ideological purposes; they may continually and regularly "leak" into other texts; but they exist for all that.

In the academic world today, however, it almost seems that this middle ground has disappeared. There are those who deny the existence of texts in any of the older senses—though they make use of their boundaries for their own convenience—and there are those who try to hang on to their older notions of sacred, autotelic structures. The physicists see things more clearly, though, for they haven't dissolved their texts (things) altogether; they've only looked at them from the other sides that they show as well. The equivalent gesture hasn't been forthcoming in the literary domain, for to make that choice would in turn mean that other decisions would have to be made, and it is always preferable to continue hovering on the edge of some perilous critical abyss.

Nietzsche made three thoroughly interconnected moves: (1) he denied the world of metaphysics and initiated a critique of its values; (2) he declared the obvious, that we are all first and foremost physical, finite creatures and attempted to revalue the world with that as a beginning and *affirmative* premise; and (3) he asserted that human existence was fundamentally aesthetic. In speaking of the need to weigh things anew, he returns us to our senses and tells us of the beauty of the aesthetic process in and through which we continually measure out the world of which we are a part. Each of these three points is simply a different way of putting the others; they are the equivalent of force equals mass times acceleration. But unlike the physicists, we have chosen not to redefine the relationship among these three factors; we have chosen the one and denied the other two, thereby defeating the entire logic of Nietzsche's enterprise.

If it were only Nietzsche's work that was at stake, we might well not be terribly concerned about the matter. We tend to take from our writers that which seems timely and leave the rest alone, and that is as it should be. But Nietzsche has been echoed in one way or another by virtually every important writer in the twentieth century, and yet we continue to insist upon our very narrow ways of reading them all—they are part of a critique, but not part of a new measurement of things. In most cases we are simply not concerned with the larger issue of revaluing the world, but even those who do nod in the direction of the new tend repeatedly to assume that they have no part in its emergence, or at least that they don't know how their work will fit into any new system of values. The best that we have to offer is a kind of Yeatsian amazement and horror at the rough beast about (perhaps) to be born, as echoed, for example, in this locution from Jacques Derrida as he ends an essay by referring to "those who, in a company from which I do not exclude myself, turn their eyes away in the face of the as yet unnameable which is proclaiming itself and which can do so, as is necessary whenever a birth is in the offing, only under the species of the non-species, in the formless, mute, infant, and terrifying form of monstrosity."[5] Derrida here boldly declares his belief that something is indeed aborning, and that, like all births, it will assuredly be monstrous; he also carefully includes himself among those who turn their eyes away from the emerging monstrosity in disgust and fear. Implicitly he is also suggesting that he himself is playing a part in causing this monstrosity to be born, but there is little sense of choice here, even less of the importance of his—or anyone's—work in seeking to bring this about. But at least something is being born, monstrous though it might be, unfathomable to us as it is.

Even if we grant to Derrida that he wrote this piece at a rather turbulent time, however, we need to ask ourselves what in the world he can be saying here. The rhetoric itself is appropriately monstrous, not simply because it obfuscates the matter entirely but more because it necessarily assumes that whatever is being born, we are bound to find it loathsome as well as aweful. But this is all too dramatic, and all too suspicious as a result. It could be that whatever is being born will indeed turn out to be monstrous, but it does not follow from what Derrida has argued that it will *inevitably* turn out that way. True to his apocalyptic ways, he *assumes* that it will be monstrous because it will by definition be radically different from anything that has come before it—how else to justify such a monstrous description? At the same time, the entire business of deconstruction shows over and over the impossibility of any such monstrosity *ever* being born. If it were to be born, it would deny our very nature, for it would totally reject everything that has come before it. It would indeed be therefore incomprehensible to us, and monstrous indeed.

Human history doesn't work that way, though. We are forever calling our predecessor the last metaphysician for precisely the reasons Heidegger and Derrida point out: it is impossible for us to escape totally from our past, and therefore it is impossible—short of nuclear oblivion—to imagine any monstrous new birth. In the end, we must assume that Derrida is doing what he does so very well: trying to act as though he hasn't chosen by arguing that the choice has already been made. The passage itself suggests large forces that will eventually overwhelm us with their monstrosity, a monstrosity that Derrida himself nevertheless chooses to help bring about. And perhaps more importantly, a monstrosity Derrida chooses to call a monstrosity. Maybe Nietzsche had it all wrong with his other two premises, but I at least choose to think that finally the monstrosity to which Derrida refers can be the result of only one of two things: our final willingness to accept our physical, finite existences and the aesthetic world of which they are a part; or our final unwillingness to accept our physical, finite existences and the aesthetic world of which they are a part. And if we finally refuse to accept our existences, I would be willing to go along with Derrida and proclaim the future monstrous birth that will occur. If this is indeed what Derrida is counseling, then he seems to be offering us nothing but despair, a wholly saleable commodity these days, but still hardly the kind of product one expects from a legitimate writer. And if Derrida is instead arguing for the more Nietzschean position, that the transvaluation of values will come about as a result of our acceptance of what we truly are, then there is no necessary reason to assume that that which is being born is monstrous. On the contrary, the very suggestion that it is monstrous denies the acceptance of human nature upon which the alternative depends. In short, this kind of utterance makes no sense either way one reads it, and although it is a grand gesture, it is the kind of locution with which we have become all too familiar, and it is finally empty and needlessly windy.

We come back, then, to the need to embrace—or at least to consider—the other two aspects of Nietzsche's thought, the two parts of his philosophy that are in the work of our poets and novelists but not in our critics. We come back to the need to arrive at a new valuation of things, a new aesthetic that measures the world in ways that are appropriate to our altered vision of things. Instead of imagining a monstrosity that is being born, we need to look at the birth that has been going on for some time; instead of refusing to go outside of the text, we need to see the text as part of the outside. We need to imagine the possibility of a fully human aesthetic, as opposed to the inhuman, metaphysical one we tried to bring to life for so many centuries. But in order to do these things, we have to reconsider the ways we look at our literature, for our present tendencies are designed to exclude that which we need in order to understand what has been emerging. And in order to do that, we must at least establish a few basic principles about what should be considered so that we have a general way of beginning.

If we assume that our new aesthetic is based upon our physicality and our finitude, several things follow. Most importantly, the distinction between the world and the text loosens considerably, as the text is as much a part of the world as it is its own distinct location. Its "thingliness" differs from other things, so it is a distinguishable field, but inasmuch as its field plays into the others of the world, the words it employs are not "unreal" at all. They are not referential in the traditional sense—the word "tree" does not point to a particular, physical tree—but the patterns the words articulate have as much reality to them as does any other pattern. This in turn means that the patterns that are articulated in literature are clear expressions of *value.* They reflect particular choices that have reference not simply to the form of a poem or a novel but also to the way lives are lived and the way the world is seen and experienced. In this way, the choices of a poem or novel don't simply contrast to other choices—rhyme, paradox, alliteration and the like—but suggest the play of choices and possibilities beyond the piece itself.

The aesthetic of physicality is one in which the choices of the writer are not simply poetic moves; they are ethical decisions within a particular form that is designed to establish a specific (if usually only implicit) system of values. This does not mean that a poem or novel is *only* an ethical system; it is above all an aesthetic domain. But the new aesthetic does not exclude ethical concerns from the poetic terrain and even goes so far as to show how intrinsic such concerns are to matters of beauty. Implicitly we always assume this to be the case anyway, so to suggest that a poem is as much an ethical system as it is an aesthetic one—or rather that it is an ethical system *because* it has a particular aesthetic—simply reintroduces aspects of the literary that have been regularly excluded from most of our criticism in the recent past.

Equally important, though, is the fact that the ethic embodied in the aesthetic is indeed always *embodied* in the aesthetic and cannot be separated from it. In contrast to the kind of political criticism we see today that turns literature into nothing more than political statements, the aesthetics of physicality must carefully delineate the precise relationship between the aesthetic and its ethical implications rather than allowing the ethics to override the aesthetic itself. Poetry is still poetry in this view of things. Its goal is not to offer prescriptive statements about the way we should live but rather to establish an aesthetic that has a pattern of perception within it that presupposes ways of making choices and experiencing existence. In this sense Auden's statement that "Poetry makes nothing happen" remains true, just as Ransom's belief that poetry has no road through to action is also correct. The ethics of literature is not narrowly conceived to generate specific results; it is instead reflected in the patterns of choice that are rendered in the text.

If we assume that literature does have an ethical component to it, we must then broaden the ways in which criticism deals with particular texts and with the tradition as a whole. It may still be important to discuss the ways in which a poem or novel relies upon works of the past, the ways in which it echoes earlier works and steals from others; it remains important to establish as best as possible the historical context of a work; and it is still useful to determine new ways of making use of the various forms available to the writer. But we must also learn how to discuss intelligently the ways in which a given piece of literature reflects a changing system of values, and not simply literary values. Likewise, we must articulate the relationship between the changing values of literature and those of other social domains—literature does not exist in its own discrete space, so to limit our discussion of it to its "literariness" is to denude it of its crucial links to the other systems that combine to articulate our sense of values.

In an earlier time, the kinds of additions to critical discussion I have been speaking of were taken up by writers with less scholarly audiences in mind. One thinks, for example, of Trilling or Wilson. Today, however, there is no such audience, at least if we are to gauge its presence from the more commercial publications. Our "high brow" magazines are decidedly low brow these days, and major presses are not seriously interested in the kind of work that writers like Trilling used to take up. But if there is no larger audience for ethical criticism anymore—and no means of disseminating such work—then it becomes the responsibility of the critics and scholars who are left behind to address the crucial ethical questions that reside in any important piece of literature, for without such work we shall see nothing but increasingly specialized writing with increasingly less attention to the connections between domains and virtually no attention at all to the ethical implications of literature.

Thus, the "outside of the text" must perforce return if we are to have any hope of removing the sterility that covers our discipline in all too many ways, and if we have any hope of doing full justice to the work of our writers, we must address the ways in which their work shapes the values through which we read them and through which we construe our own lives. The range of our interests must expand to embrace the interests of our writers without at the same time reducing all of them to a narrow grid of expectations and outcomes. Whatever form such a criticism might take, it ought not to be based upon a kind of prescriptivism that determines beforehand the proper values for a given writer. It may be true that we come to any text with our own values and expectations already in place, and it may be true that we read these expectations into the text at hand, but we are also capable to a large extent of separating our expectations from what a given text actually offers us. In the end we inevitably decide upon the efficacy of a particular text for our own ways of construing things, and thus pass judgment upon the values that it establishes, but at the same time we need to recognize that any text has its own mass, force and velocity that are more or less discernible.

Our writers have been in the process of establishing anew the weights of things for some time now, and they have gone a long way toward articulating a newer, more wholly human vision of the world even as we have increasingly retreated into our endless discussions of the things that words do. From Whitman's time to the present we have seen many writers who affirm the value of life at the same time that they have cautiously appraised the impediments to our future, and it is time that we began properly to measure the new possibilities with which they have presented us. And if the world remains hedged about with the limits of what we have already done and what we can never do, there is still a literary region that exists between those limits that doesn't resort to the apocalyptic monstrosities we have become enamored of or the despair that we seek to avoid by imagining a radical new birth. This is a less glamorous region, to be sure, but perhaps its quiet and careful affirmations have more value in the end precisely because they relate to the minutiae of everyday life and continue to establish possibilities for us in the contingent world of which we are always only a part. Fortunately, our poets and novelists have not always been so willing to follow the drift toward irony; unfortunately, we ironize them even when they seek to value. We strip them of their courage in order to feel better about ourselves. But their voices are still in the background, and it doesn't take much effort to hear them if one is inclined to listen.

. . . .

In the American tradition, there are many voices that clearly attest to the ethical force of literature, but for my purposes three writers from three different periods best serve to exemplify what can and cannot be said about the ethical nature of writing: Walt Whitman, Wallace Stevens and A. R. Ammons. Whitman may be a Romantic, Stevens a Modernist and Ammons a contemporary poet, but their work shares an interest in the relationship between values and poetry. This relationship is most obvious in Whitman, for a poem like "Song of Myself" proclaims from beginning to end a fresh way of looking at the world, but Stevens and Ammons are equally compelled to articulate an ethical vision of life. Stevens' work may seem to be far more interested in epistemological or ontological questions than ethical ones, and in many respects this is indeed the case, but in some of his best poems—particularly "Esthétique du Mal"—the question of value is paramount. Ammons, who follows more obviously in the Whitmanian line—and who also has a fairly clear interest in environmental questions and the like—demonstrates to us the ways in which our current thinking about the ethical can be satisfactorily integrated into a poetics of great richness and complexity.

Inasmuch as Whitman, Stevens and Ammons are simply representative figures, my discussion of their work makes no attempt to be comprehensive, nor does it seek to engage the various critical debates that have evolved around their poetry. Likewise, my selection of their poems is brief: "Song of Myself" for Whitman; "The Idea of Order at Key West," "Of Modern Poetry" and "Esthétique du Mal" for Stevens; and "Essay on Poetics" and "Corsons Inlet" for Ammons. These poems are central to each writer's work, and they are also central to any understanding of American poetry and its relation to the ethical, so they will serve as admirable reflections of the questions that are inevitably raised when the problem of value and poetry arises.

Chapter One

WHITMAN'S AFFIRMATION OF THE WORLD

In the American tradition, there is no poet who had a broader vision of the value of literature than Walt Whitman, and even if there are aspects of his vision that seem a bit outmoded in the twentieth century, the striking thing is how consonant so much of his work still is. Whitman may believe a bit too strongly in what has come to be called the Adamic myth, and may thus be justly accused of having a nostalgic vision of the world, but his nostalgia is always tempered by his awareness of the way the world in fact is. One of the virtues of "Song of Myself" as a poetic statement is that it always manages to include those aspects of existence we don't expect it to—just as Whitman seems to have taken his nostalgia as far as it will go, he brings us back to the other side of life, the one that all too many Romantic poets exclude altogether.

In the first section of "Song of Myself," for example, Whitman tells us that he has put "Creeds and schools in abeyance, / Retiring back a while sufficed at what they are, but never forgotten,"[1] and explains that "I harbor for good or bad, I permit to speak at every hazard, / Nature without check with original energy" (12,13). Such a statement can be easily critiqued today, when one need only point out that humans are incapable of expressing "Nature without check" or with "original energy"; in us "nature" is always checked by the means through which we perceive it, and its original energy can never be discerned by humans simply because they are in culture. As we find throughout the poem, though, Whitman has tempered this statement by the way in which he talks about the "Creeds and schools" he has put in abeyance. Unlike those who would argue that such structures can be dispensed with, he realizes that the best he can do is momentarily hold them in abeyance, and even then he knows that they are "never forgotten." But if this is so, it must surely affect the way in which nature is articulated with original energy and call into question the degree to which nature can be expressed without check.

Whitman, of course, waits until the very end of the poem to state "Do I contradict myself? / Very well then I contradict myself" (1324,25), but he seems to have been doing that from the very beginning, as we see in his articulation of the relationship between creeds and natural energy. How can one both accept that creeds are never forgotten and have hope of expressing the natural energy of the world? If the creeds are not forgotten, then they must affect in some respects the ways we perceive things, even if they are held in abeyance, so they must restrict the natural energy we have within us. And if that is the case, then humans can never get back to any kind of natural energy simply because it is always held in check by the creeds and schools through which they construe the world. Whitman has indeed contradicted himself, and he offers no resolution of this enigma. We can say that he is simply being naive here, or we can look for another kind of explanation.

If we keep in mind that Whitman has made his task more difficult by conceding that creeds are never forgotten, we must also wonder why he didn't just forget about them altogether. He could have suggested that he was capable of transcending the creeds, of returning to an original relationship with the natural world that ignored the structures of society altogether. Instead, he willingly admits that he can no more escape the confines of society than anyone else can, yet he insists that he can still express the original energy of nature. Within his own poetics, he can accomplish this because he deliberately violates the law of non-contradiction: he asserts that he contradicts himself and explains that he has no problem with that. He is a contradictory thing himself—just as the world is—and he sees no reason to be consistent when doing so would violate his conception of his nature. Further, when he concedes that he contradicts himself, he justifies it by saying "(I am large, I contain multitudes)" (1326), as though that would resolve the difficulty. As far as Whitman is concerned, his multitudinousness does indeed resolve the problem, for he realizes that the unity of himself—and his poem—does not depend upon a foolish consistency that makes logical sense while denying the complexity of human nature. Even if there are large portions of his being that are irretrievably connected to the check of creeds, there are other parts that are still capable of expressing nature without check, and if this sounds strange to us, there is no reason to think Whitman is wrong in saying so.

Whitman does contradict himself, and he seems to be asserting the possibility of an original contact with the natural world as well, something that we have long since abandoned. But it seems entirely logical in its own way for Whitman to assert this original contact, even if it defies logic. We might be willing, for example, to concede the issue when it is cast in a slightly different light, as when the natural energy is expressed as rage rather than joy. Surely those people who are susceptible every now and then to "irrational" rages are in some important ways reflecting their own kind of natural energy, and surely that energy is not held in check by creeds and schools. If it were, the person would by definition *control* his anger and thereby avoid becoming so irrational. In a real way, an irrational rage is nothing more (or less) than the expression of natural energy—creeds and schools have been held in abeyance, though not forgotten, and the rage simply plays itself out. One could, I suppose, argue that an irrational rage is somehow based on a nostalgic desire for the origin, but it seems more logical simply to assert that such a rage overpowers the social structures through which humans usually control their anger.

If the rage is not "pure," if it is "corrupted" by creeds in some way, that is less important than the fact that it is an all too "natural" response to certain situations. We are large, we contain multitudes, and sometimes parts of our multiplicity surprise us by their appearance and their force. One cannot reconcile a rage to one's more typical, orderly behavior, for the one contradicts the other. But they do both exist in the same person, so we must accept the fact that human behavior is not logical and that it does not subscribe to our facile notions of unity. And if we can say such things about an irrational rage, why can't we say the same kinds of things about the natural exuberance that Whitman expresses throughout the poem? He is not violating any basic premises of human nature. Far from it. He is expressing the naturally contradictory nature of all humans. And he does not use his natural exuberance to deny the force of social structures, to imagine himself into another world, so he can hardly be accused of seeking to avoid the constraints of everyday life. He is simply trying to place those constraints in a larger context, and that is precisely what a poem like "Song of Myself" does.

Whitman's stance is disconcerting to us in part because it violates the ways we have come to think of ourselves, but this does not mean that he has it wrong. Perhaps we do. "Song of Myself," we know, is a poem that celebrates Whitman—"I celebrate myself, and sing myself"—and it is unified by the self that Whitman is. But this self, so full of multiplicity, hardly conforms to our usual notions of unity in multiplicity, for we tend to reduce the multiplicity to a unity while Whitman avoids doing so. He is a multiplicity, and that multiplicity is unified to the extent that it bears the name "Whitman," but all of his urges and tendencies don't come together into an identity any more than the paradoxes of his nature resolve themselves. The unity is *loose* rather than tight, and this difference makes Whitman's conception of self considerably different from ours.

The modern world tends to see selfhood in the way New Critics saw poems: the unity of identity is achieved through the tension of the paradoxical elements of the personality. These elements somehow magically tend toward an equilibrium that brings all the forces together. I. A. Richards told us that it was literature's function to help us achieve that kind of equilibrium, as though the paradoxes of our nature could somehow be canceled out into a mystical unification of opposites, as though homoestasis would be achieved by a magical mixture of the tensions within us. But Whitman doesn't see his complexity that way at all. The tensions and paradoxes within him don't resolve themselves. They can't. They all exist within that one person, Whitman, but there is no homeostasis, no equilibrium that brings all the elements together to form the perfectly unified blend that Whitman would like to imagine as his self. The various aspects of his being remain discrete yet connected; they do not reduce to a simple unity any more than they disperse into a thousand fragments. And if modern readers want to impose their own superficial notions of unified identities upon Whitman, they are misreading his conception of what it means to be human. Likewise, if post-structuralist readers want to speak of the death and dispersion of the self and Whitman's failure to acknowledge this change, they are ignoring the very real, if multiplicitous, densities that human beings are.

One gets a different sense of the way in which Whitman sees human existence—and yet another angle on the problem of human contradiction—in the fourth stanza of "Song of Myself" where he explains to us what he is in considerable detail:

> Trippers and askers surround me,
>
> People I meet, the effect upon me of my early life or the ward and city I live in, or the nation,
>
> The latest dates, discoveries, inventions, societies, authors old and new,
>
> My dinner, dress, associates, looks, compliments, dues,
>
> The real or fancied indifference of some man or woman I love,
>
> The sickness of one of my folks or of myself, or ill-doing or loss or lack of money, or depressions or exaltations,

Battles, the horrors of fratricidal war, the fever of doubtful news, the fitful events;

These come to me days and nights and go from me again,

But they are not the Me myself.

Apart from the pulling and hauling stands what I am,

Stands amused, complacent, compassionating, idle, unitary,

Looks down, is erect, or bends an arm on an impalpable certain rest,

Looking with side-curved head curious what will come next,

Both in and out of the game and watching and wondering at it.

Backward I see in my own days where I sweated through fog with linguists and contenders,

I have no mockings or arguments, I witness and wait. (66–81)

In the first half of this stanza, Whitman does a fairly comprehensive job of cataloging the various ways through which we come to define our selves. He begins with the people he knows, the effects of his childhood upon him, and the ways in which his location in a particular ward, city and nation have helped to define him. From there he turns to "The latest dates, discoveries, inventions, societies, authors old and new" that have helped further establish his sense of self. In a poem whose first half is devoted to the poet breathing in the entire world, it is not surprising that Whitman would find everything from discoveries and inventions to the ideas of all the writers he has encountered to have affected the way he construes himself. These are important ways through which we come to articulate the intangible aspects of our existence, and they are precisely described here.

In addition to these factors, Whitman acknowledges the role that his social life plays in defining him, listing everything from his food to the way he dresses to the people with whom he associates and the ways in which they respond to him—these social interactions reinforce some aspects of his life and deny others and thereby help to shape him. Similarly, from worries about our relatives to concerns about money, from the normal cycle of depressions and exaltations to the larger social upheavals like war and other "fitful events," our lives continue to be articulated by those things around us that continually affect the way we look at the world, and hence at ourselves.

In the twentieth century—and doubtless the nineteenth as

well—this list of "external" effects details most of the ways we make sense of ourselves and is thus designed to prompt us to agree with the effects such things have. But Whitman lists these items so elaborately only so he can tell us at the end that "These come to me days and nights and go from me again, / But they are not the Me myself." He sweeps all these effects away with one stroke, thereby denying our conventional definitions of selfhood. The problem with this move from a modern perspective, however, is that it seems to set up an essential self that exists outside of the social and physical worlds—the "Me myself," with its capital "M," suggests a transcendent being that is not affected by the turmoil, strife and joys of everyday life. In the post-existential world where existence precedes essence, such a definition of self simply won't do, and at this point the reader is inclined to back away from the purified vision that Whitman is offering here.

Although our view of this purified self will become more complex as the stanza proceeds, Whitman insists on this essential vision of himself in the next line when he explains that "Apart from the pulling and hauling stands what I am." Again, the contrast between the self as defined by the "pulling and hauling" of everyday life and the essential self that stands apart from life could not be made any more clearly. We are meant to believe at this point that the poet is simply not affected by all those things that we know affect us; or rather, his sense of self is not affected by the pulling and hauling. Instead, Whitman's idealized self is capable of a transcendent perspective that removes him from the world. He "Stands amused, complacent, compassionating, idle, unitary," measuring his distance from the turmoil of existence by the words he uses to describe his own point of view. Far from being distressed by those things that happen in the social world, this idealized self is amused, observing what goes on from a distance that makes the pettiness of everything seem rather silly. This self can thus be complacent about its own participation in life at the same time that it can be "compassionating" toward those who are caught up in the struggle.

The idleness to which the poet refers here in turn suggests a different kind of orientation toward the experiences of everyday life, the kind of perspective laid out at the very beginning of the poem when Whitman exclaimed "I lean and loafe at my ease" (5). As with the word "idle," "loafe" manages to explain the change in viewpoint in several ways. First, inasmuch as "America" is built upon the work ethic, loafing is looked down upon, so by choosing this word, Whitman manages to establish his disdain for what the workers of the world might feel about him at the same time that he makes clear his indifference to their attitudes. More importantly, loafing is meant to contrast with those characteristics that go along with the work ethic: an intensely focused vision of things that centers everything on the self and self-promotion. Far from adopting this narrow viewpoint, Whitman chooses a broader, non-focused perspective, one that allows him to see things as they come to him, one that doesn't organize everything in the world according to the expectations of the observer. He is simply idly standing by, loafing around and watching what comes next. It is not that he is doing nothing; far from it. Rather, his vision is broad enough for him to see the processes of the world in a different way, a way that minimizes the degree to which his own forceful desire to act affects things.

This expanded vision of the purer self is elaborated on further in the next lines, where we are told that it "Looks down, is erect, or bends an arm on an impalpable certain rest, / Looking with side-curved head curious what will come next." The poet changes his angle of vision as it occurs to him to do so, looking down or standing erect as the occasion seems to warrant, but underlying all of his choices is the sense of his arm leaning on "an impalpable certain rest." To others it may look as though his arm is hanging in the air, for its resting place is impalpable, but even if that which it leans on is not visible, it still offers a "certain rest," one that is totally sure in its feel. The curiosity of the poet's vision, that which allows him to have such an expansive view, is based upon the surety of this certain rest, for that is the ground that allows him to be curious and disinterested when others would be adopting more partial, interested, involved attitudes. Only by removing himself from the everyday sense of existence can Whitman see what his real "Me myself" is.

By this point in the stanza, the modern reader thinks he has caught Whitman in the midst of the Romantic nostalgia for a grounded, essential self, one that transcends the world and provides an all-encompassing view of things that allows the poet to rise above the status of mere mortal. From the "Me myself" to the "impalpable certain rest," Whitman seems quite clearly to have been detailing a view of the self as a pure being that remains uncontaminated by its experiences in the world, and the result is that the poem itself begins to sound in its own way like a Wordsworthian attempt to recover a former self that was lost when the speaker moved into the social world of adulthood. The only thing in these lines that works against that view of Whitman is that he offers us no sense of loss, and hence provides no reason for an act of recovery. Far from being based on the view that "The things which I have seen I now can see no more," "Song of Myself" begins and ends with the impression that the poet has never had such a fall—he has always been able to see what he sees now and hence has no need to recover an earlier state of grace. The absence of a sense of loss in the poem might be enough to convince the reader that perhaps Whitman is not being nostalgic, and at least it should be enough to demonstrate that he is not being nostalgic in the conventional way. Still, one is left with the impression that Whitman's view of self is all too rarefied.

Having undercut the conventional vision of self, Whitman seems content to live with the illusion of a purified self instead, but just as we are accommodating ourselves to this view, he complicates matters by telling us that he is "Both in and out of the game and watching and wondering at it." It seems up to this point that the first half of the stanza provides a perspective that illustrates an "in-the-game" view of the world while the second half provides us with an "out-of-the-game" perspective. After all, from the modern viewpoint the problem with the second section is precisely that it argues that there *is* an out-of-the-game perspective when we no longer believe there is one. If there is no outside of the text, there is no outside of the game either. But now Whitman tells us that he is both in the game *and* out of it, so we are forced once again to revise our conception of what he has been telling us about his view of selfhood.

As Whitman suggested at the beginning of the poem when he stated that he had only put creeds and schools in abeyance, here too we find that he has never denied that he is in the game as much as anyone else is. Much later in the poem this is confirmed again when the poet tells us:

> This is the city and I am one of the citizens,
>
> Whatever interests the rest interest me, politics, wars, markets, newspapers, schools,
>
> The mayor and councils, banks, tariffs, steamships, factories, stocks, stores, real estate and personal estate. (1075–77)

Whitman no more denies that he is a part of the "pulling and hauling" of everyday life than he disavows being human. Nor is Whitman distressed by this fact; on the contrary, he loves being in the game as much as he values being out of it. He is not only interested and curious about the things that go on in the social world; he also wants actively to participate in them. Whitman clearly relishes the contact of society as much as he loves the air of the natural world. Indeed, he tells us that "Houses and rooms are full of perfumes, the shelves are crowded with perfumes, / I breathe the fragrance myself and know it and like it, / The distillation would intoxicate me also, but I shall not let it" (14–16). It takes a considerable act of self-control on Whitman's part to keep from being overwhelmed by the "perfumes" and "rooms" of the social world, but he realizes that he would lose something great if his world were reduced to nothing more than these social fragrances.

At the same time, Whitman also recognizes the nature of the social world, most tellingly here by speaking of it in terms of a "game." Like a game, society is built up out of arbitrary rules, conventions that are accepted as "real" but which are artificial for all that. Like a game, the social world is based upon the "pulling and hauling" for arbitrary rewards that have little intrinsic value in themselves. Like a game, one must play it as though everything in it is indeed real, meaningful and significant. And at least from the traditional perspective, it is precisely the ability to recognize that society is for all practical purposes a game-like structure that allows one to be out of the game as well. Those totally within it fail to see it as a game. They take it for reality and believe in the veracity of the rules and the viability of the outcomes. They strive within the range of their narrow goals to achieve what society calls a meaningful existence, never realizing that the value of what they achieve is based from the beginning on arbitrary assumptions about what is and isn't real. But if Whitman is capable of realizing all these things, he is also more than willing to partake of the game, both because he enjoys it and because he is intent upon accepting what it means to be fully human.

In contrast, when Whitman is out of the game he is adopting a different perspective, variously characterized in terms of loafing or watching with side-curved head. His vision is expanded rather than narrowed; he sees how the game-like structure of society is encompassed by the larger rhythms of the natural world of which it is always only a part. And from this angle, the poet can appreciate the insignificance of the stakes within the social game even as he can see better the way things are heading within society. This larger, aesthetic vision allows the poet to see the relationships between things that aren't perceivable within the narrower domain and also lets him see his own place within both frameworks.

There are two problems with this perspective from a modern point of view, though, and again both of them have to do with the possibility of achieving it. It may well be that in contrast to other Romantic poets, Whitman does not reject society but embraces it; it may well be that he wants to be both in and out of the game. But we need to ask if there is an "out-of-the-game," just as we need to ask about the temporal relationship between being in and out of it. When Whitman tells us that he is both in and out of the game, does he mean to suggest that he is both in and out *at the same time*? If so, we need to ask if it is truly possible to be both in and out at the same time. Isn't it perhaps the case that the best one can expect is something of a dialectic between the two? Isn't it impossible finally to imagine combining both perspectives at the same time? Whitman never insists upon the simultaneity of these two visions, but it seems that that is indeed what he suggests. If so, the reader can't help but wonder if this statement is false, at least in its precise implications.

The temporal problem is only a manifestation of the larger question of whether or not it is possible truly to be out of the game. Our current ways of thinking deny this possibility. At best one could say today that one changes games, not that one escapes the game altogether. And if we revise Whitman in this way, we in turn then have to point out that once one concedes that there is only a choice between games, there is no definitive way of establishing the superiority of one game over another. Both would by definition have arbitrary rules, goals and procedures, so the choice of one or the other would be an expression of value, but not an expression of definitive value. *Is* there an out of the game, then, or is Whitman deluding himself?

In Whitman's defense, we can say that even if there is no "pure" out of the game, there is something that might indeed resemble this state; that even if there is no definitive way of establishing the value of this game, it does seem to transcend human conceptions of it. That is, the natural world is in one sense a game in itself simply because we always perceive it through our knowledge of it, and this knowledge is always partial and hence arbitrary. "Nature," as we say today, is only another sign, and so it is only another game with no special privileges attached to it simply because we have valorized this sign for millennia. But there are things within this natural world that have been observed by countless people over millennia too, and this suggests that the "rules" of this game are not arbitrary in the same sense the social rules are. They are arbitrary because they are incomplete, but they are real in that we cannot change them. Within a social structure we can always theoretically choose to be governed by kings or presidents; we can choose to value one way of life over another, and these changes in the rules can be put into effect, at least over time. Within the natural world, though, there is no changing the rules. We can modify our understanding of them, but we can't alter them. One way or the other, living creatures must eat in order to remain alive; they must die eventually; they must participate in processes of life and death that far transcend their own concern for existence; and they need in some way to accommodate these facts, however they are construed. And this suggests clearly that if one can't be totally out of the game, the other context to which Whitman refers is indeed something more than just another game. Its rules take precedence over any human game in the end, and so in a real way the natural world is "out of the game."

Whitman's declaration that he is both in and out of the game must thus be seen in two ways. On the one hand, he does indeed mean that there are two views of the world, and while he embraces both, he clearly values the social game in terms of the natural world through which he construes it. In this sense the natural world is out of the game for him; it is the ground through which he gives value to the things of his life. On the other hand, though, it is indeed possible to be both in and out of the game at the same time. That is precisely what our understanding of the natural world is inasmuch as it always involves at the same time a partial rendering of the "laws" of nature—hence it is in the game—and a response to certain immutable facts about human existence—hence it is out of the game. This is the aesthetic upon which "Song of Myself" is finally based, as we see again and again throughout the poem, and if it is contradictory, Whitman has no problem with that.

When Whitman declares at the end of the poem that he *too* is "untranslatable," he is demonstrating the ways in which his poem is both in and out of the game. In its entirety it has been, in one sense, devoted to expressing what and who Whitman is; it is designed to articulate the "Me myself." Yet at the end Whitman confesses that the "Me myself" is still outside of the poem. Even more, by using the word "too" in this line, he argues that everything else he has been talking about is also finally untranslatable—he has tried to show us the natural processes of which we are all a part, but he has had to do so in an arbitrary way, via his own imperfect conceptions and the imperfections of the social games involved in language and the construction of poetry. The "Me myself" and the natural world might both be seen as the "supplement" that is both more and less than it purports to be in the skeptical modern fashion, or they might be seen simply as active forces that are always in the process of change, *real* forces that can only be partially articulated by the arbitrariness of language. We are perhaps too easily convinced that the forces that are in—yet always manage to escape—a poem are mere figments of a nostalgic imagination, but it remains the case that however much we choose to deny a location outside of the game, and however we choose to construe the natural world, its rules are always capable of overriding our foolishness in denying them and inevitably they always will.

Whitman himself addresses this problem throughout "Song of Myself," and perhaps one of his best statements on the matter comes toward the end of the poem when he delineates for the reader what the goals of the poem are:

> But each man and each woman of you I lead upon a knoll,
>
> My left hand hooking you round the waist,
>
> My right hand pointing to landscapes of continents and the public road. (1207–09)

In contrast to the transcendental visions of other poets, those marvelous confections that occur on mountaintops, Whitman concedes that he does no more than lead us upon a knoll. He may have been showing us what the world looks like when one is out of the game, but he doesn't believe for a moment that he has transcended the earth. Far from it. The best he can do is lead us to a knoll, giving us a larger perspective of things, but one that is also fully rooted in the earth and the things around us. Whitman's "out of the game," then, is not out of this world; it is *in* this world, even if he defines the world as both a social and a natural scene.

In the same vein, Whitman tells us what he has been showing us all along, and that consists of "landscapes of continents and the public road." In the game and out of it as always, he has pointed to the landscapes of continents, given us the larger vision of the natural world that we inhabit, and he has also gestured in the direction of the public road, embracing both of the aspects of human existence at the same time. We see over and over again in the poem that while it is the natural world—the world of continents and the earth as a whole—that provides the perspective through which to perceive the social world of the public road, the two remain inseparable. The one takes precedence over the other, but for humans the two are inextricably combined, and Whitman no more wants us to deny one aspect of our beings than he wants us to deny the other. He celebrates both with equal enthusiasm because life is composed of both.

Nevertheless, it remains true that any skeptical reading of the poem—and of the possibility of being both in and out of the game—would find Whitman's logic to be flawed and contradictory. For some readers this is eventually an overriding issue, and in such cases Whitman's work fails because even if he acknowledges the flaws in his argument, he still chooses to embrace it. From Whitman's perspective, it is clearly more important to provide as comprehensive a view of human existence as possible than to be logically consistent. If he is forced to sacrifice a common-sensical view of things for the richness of his texture, he will obligingly do so. This is where he differs from the skeptical reader, for he chooses complexity and richness (and inconsistency) over the consistency of the skeptical view. He chooses to value some things over others on the basis of what he feels to be true even as he acknowledges that he has no godlike insight into things any more than we do. He is on a knoll, not a mountaintop, and he is not the least bit embarrassed to tell us so.

The difference between Whitman's perspective and the skeptical vision of things is best expressed in the problems inherent in being both in and out of the game, for the contradictory nature of that statement contrasts very well with the skeptical tendency toward irony. An ironist would take Whitman's statement and turn it on itself. Not only would this move demonstrate the impossibility of being both in and out of the game, but it would also point out the impossibility of choosing one of the perspectives over the other: to choose to be in the game is to deny the value of being out of it, and vice versa. The result would be that the ironist would choose neither view, denying the possibility of being out of the game, scorning the value of being in the game. Caught within that grid, the individual would be incapable of meaningful choice—all that would be left would be the continual undercutting of the rules of the game, the never-ending articulations of the ways in which we are deceived by—and deceive—through the artificial rules of social structures.

Whitman, in contrast, chooses *both* possibilities, accepting at the same time the contradictoriness of being able to do so. Instead of being bothered by the fact that his position is logically impossible, he asserts its necessity all the same. In turn, this perspective allows him to see the artificiality of the rules of the game without at the same time denying the necessity of participating in it anyway. And because he also has an out-of-the-game view, he is capable of seeing the rules for what they are and can try to change them in ways that are consonant with the larger laws of the natural world of which he is also a part. Whitman's world is thus one that is filled with value and with the need to choose that which is most appropriate to his context, and these choices are precisely what Whitman relishes most.

. . . . . .

While the ironist denies the possibility of value and diminishes thereby the importance of any particular choice, Whitman's vision allows him to assert that the world is value-*full*, even if the values are imperfect expressions of human choice, and the play between the in-the-game and out-of-the-game visions allows him continually to make better-informed choices. He chooses the smelly armpits *and* the glory of language; he accepts his nature, both good and bad, and assesses the world from that vantage point rather than trying to deny that one thing can be valued over another. And because Whitman is willing to learn from everything he experiences, his range of choice is not limited by those things society as a whole considers off limits: "Welcome is every organ and attribute of me, and of any man hearty and clean, / Not an inch nor a particle of an inch is vile, and none shall be less familiar than the rest" (57,58). He embraces everything that humanity is rather than restricting himself to those things the rules of the game insist he should concentrate on.

The value of Whitman's aesthetic is established upon a rejection of the traditional rules of society in two ways. First, his willingness to embrace a logically contradictory position denies him the comforts available to those who seek above all for a kind of consistency. In the twentieth-century world, this means that the skeptic finds his views to be hopelessly flawed and nostalgic. But second, his perspective also denies the value of the nostalgic vision he is accused of having. Those who adhere to the pieties of Western metaphysics—those who still wish for a transcendental vision of the world—also find Whitman's views flawed because he denies the value of those pieties and forces the pious to focus on what *is* rather than on what they desire. The larger issue here is best expressed by Whitman's acknowledgment of the way he parts company with the metaphysicians:

> I heard what was said of the universe,
>
> Heard it and heard it of several thousand years;
>
> It is middling well as far as it goes—but is that all?
>
>
> Magnifying and applying come I,
>
> Outbidding at the start the old cautious hucksters,
>
> Taking myself the exact dimensions of Jehovah,
>
> Lithographing Kronos, Zeus his son, and Hercules his grandson,

Buying drafts of Osiris, Isis, Belus, Brahma, Buddha,

In my portfolio placing Manito loose, Allah on a leaf, the crucifix engraved,

With Odin and the hideous-faced Mexitli and every idol and image,

Taking them all for what they are worth and not a cent more,

Admitting they were alive and did the work of their days . . .

Accepting the rough deific sketches to fill out better in myself . . .

Discovering as much or more in a framer framing a house. . . .
(1023–38)

Whitman is well aware of his opposition simply because the complaints to be leveled at his view have been heard "of several thousand years." He devotes himself exclusively to the universe, to *this* world, and has no intention of figuring forth another world beyond this one. For him, the world we have is more than enough, totally satisfying and as full as one could want it.

But the majority of humans don't agree with Whitman. The best they can conjure is the notion that "It is middling well as far as it goes—but is that all?" They seem to want more than this universe and believe that their desires can only be properly fulfilled if they have still another world to fill in the lacks of this one. So even if such individuals would grant to Whitman that there are indeed delights to be had on this planet, that there is joy and the world is good, it is always only more or less good, and because there is also grief, and evil, and death, the universe is never enough to satisfy them. Whitman nonetheless subtly shows the foolishness of the dream of another world in this passage simply by stating "I heard what was said of the universe." This complaint against the universe has been heard for thousands of years, and in every case it comes from individuals who are such a microcosmically small part of the world that their complaint is almost a cosmic joke—that they should have complaints against a thing so vast and large is the final absurdity, small and insignificant as they are. Of course it is precisely that sense of smallness and insignificance that rankles those who wish for another world and prevents them from seeing the perfections in this one.

True to form, though, Whitman does not reject the great religions and religious figures of the past just because he refuses to imagine another world in which to live. He "outbid[s] at the start the old cautious hucksters" who want to keep humans dissatisfied with their present world by conjuring up nostalgic visions from the great gods of the past by "Taking [him]self the exact dimensions of Jehovah," by measuring for himself the value of each of the great religious icons of the past. He even goes further than the typical Westerner by including the gods of all major civilizations, from Kronos to Osiris to Brahma and Buddha. And in measuring each of these past gods, he is willing to sort the valuable from the valueless, "Taking them all for what they are worth and not a cent more." Each god has value for Whitman to the extent that he represents a displaced embodiment of human desires and ideals, and so he can accept their "rough deific sketches to fill out better" himself, incorporating a larger human vision out of the seemingly inhuman vision of each of these figures.

Whitman admits that all of these gods "were alive and did the work of their days," but in saying so he also argues that it was the work of *their* days, that their time is past. We can learn from their visions of human desire, but they are part of a world that is gone because in Whitman's view we have arrived at the point where we can accept the universe for what it is, just as we can accept our place within it for what it is. While not denying the value of the gods, then, Whitman diminishes it in traditional terms and emphasizes this shift by concluding that he discovers "as much or more in a framer framing a house." The choice of a framer is important inasmuch as he works in this world building houses for human beings out of the materials around him instead of building an ideal world with fictive materials. And the framer is also important because he is working, creating the world in which we live and will come to live. His talents are godlike in their own way precisely because they allow him to create the new within the never-ending process of the universe.

In choosing to be both in and out of the game, then, Whitman has one chief problem: he has denied the value of both the skeptical and the nostalgic visions and asserted a radically different position that can be easily denied from either of the other perspectives. Even more, he recognizes that he has done so and boldly proclaims his difference. True to the paradoxical nature of "Song of Myself," though, Whitman also has a profound faith that even if he is denying the value of the prevailing views, his readers will still recognize the truth in what he is saying. Repeatedly he reminds us that he thinks he is speaking for all of us, as when he admits that:

> These are really the thoughts of all men in all ages and lands, they are
> not original with me,

> If they are not yours as much as mine they are nothing, or next to
> nothing,
>
> If they are not the riddle and the untying of the riddle they are
> nothing,
>
> If they are not just as close as they are distant they are nothing.
>
> This is the grass that grows wherever the land is and the water is,
>
> This is the common air that bathes the globe. (355–360)

Whitman is simply breathing in "the common air that bathes the globe" and exhaling it again in the form of poetry, and if his thoughts "are not [ours] as much as [his] they are nothing." If we do not at some level immediately recognize the truth of what he is telling us, then what he says has no value at all because he is writing about the way things are in the universe. He is not articulating a private vision in which we can all participate; he is expressing a public vision that depends upon our assent for its validity.

It is equally important to note that Whitman therefore has no aggrandized vision of himself or his work. He recognizes that he is expressing the "thoughts of all men in all ages and lands," and by admitting that "they are not original with me" he is demystifying his role as poet. He is not some special creature who, Kronos-like, is capable of seeing things the rest of us cannot; on the contrary, what he sees has been seen by all humans of all ages. If there is a difference to Whitman it is that he has chosen to act on the basis of what he sees rather than what he desires, thereby refusing to deny what all humans already know, and this clearly changes the way one looks at the knowledge we all possess. But Whitman is only repeating what has been said for millennia, simply reinforcing a knowledge of the universe of which we are all aware, even if we act against that knowledge rather than with it. The problem the poem faces is that we don't want to admit that Whitman's vision is accurate because it forces us to accept what we should prefer to avoid; the courage of the poem in this sense is that it assumes humans are perhaps finally capable of accepting what they have known for thousands of years, are now willing to learn to live in the only world they have.

The gap between knowledge and desire is the space that Whitman seeks to fill out, even as he is aware of the contradictions in which that will involve him. And if those contradictions appear when he asserts the necessity for being both in and out of the game, they appear even larger when one sees the framework out of which that necessity arises. Out of the game, the universe appears far different than it does within it, and Whitman speaks to that contrast early on:

> I have heard what the talkers were talking, the talk of the beginning and the end,
>
> But I do not talk of the beginning or the end.
>
> There was never any more inception than there is now,
>
> Nor any more youth or age than there is now,
>
> And will never be any more perfection than there is now,
>
> Nor any more heaven or hell than there is now.
>
> Urge and urge and urge,
>
> Always the procreant urge of the world.
>
> Out of the dimness opposite equals advance, always substance and increase, always sex,
>
> Always a knit of identity, always distinction, always a breed of life. (38–46)

Well aware of America's regularly apocalyptic tendencies, and even more aware of the American obsession with beginnings and ends in general, Whitman clearly distinguishes his view from the norm by declaring "I do not talk of the beginning or the end." In contrast to the linear perspective that is always promising some kind of reward (or punishment) at the end, Whitman's vision is decidedly cyclical and denies the appropriateness of conceiving of our lives in linear terms. Granted, virtually all of the social structures are configured in this manner; nevertheless the world Whitman sees denies that linearity at every level. As he tells us, "There was never any more inception than there is now, / Nor any more youth or age than there is now, / And will never be any more perfection than there is now." The poet has no sympathy with the traditional vision that prompts one to deny the present by wishing for a better future, either in a personal or a social way—one's life is always as perfect as it is ever going to be, and the social world will never be any more perfect either. In focusing resolutely on the perfections of the moment, Whitman thus reinscribes the world so that we are able to move away from our obsessions with the past and future.

The world will never be any more perfect than it is at present simply because its processes are always the same: "Urge and urge and urge, / Always the procreant urge of the world." Inasmuch as the procreative urge doesn't grow or diminish, there is no reason to think that things were once better, or that they will be better in the future. The world is urge, nothing more and nothing less, and the beauty and perfection that arise from that urge are always present and available to anyone willing to look for them within his present circumstances. In turn Whitman describes the process of the urge of life in the following way: "Out of the dimness opposite equals advance, always substance and increase, always sex, / Always a knit of identity, always distinction, always a breed of life." The emphasis on the urge of the world and the present leads him to focus on the physical, sexual ways in which substance and increase occur, reminding us of the basic bodily processes through which the urge of the world manifests itself, but he is also speaking about more than sex when he refers to the opposite equals advancing out of the dimness. As Whitman explains later in the poem, he cannot trace things back behind that dimness to an origin, but he does know that the substance and increase of sex were there from the beginning just as he knows that the substance and increase occur precisely because there are always opposite *equals* advancing. In contrast to the social world where the master/slave relationship often dominates, within the natural world the opposing forces are always equal, as they must be if the world is to generate the productivity necessary for its perpetuation. Likewise, the "breed of life" is equally based on the "knit of identity" and the necessary distinction that arises from that unified whole. Distinction is that through which the world generates the new, is that through which the urge of the world ceaselessly expresses itself, and this accounts for the heavy commitment Whitman makes throughout the poem to the new, that most recent distinction that rewrites the sense of everything that comes before it.

In emphasizing the sexual nexus out of which all of our urges arise, though, and in emphasizing that there will never be any more perfection than there is now—in demonstrating that talk of the beginning and end is foolish—Whitman clearly denies the major threads of Western discourse. At this point in the poem he seems much more closely aligned with the Eastern tradition and its emphasis on the illusion of progress. Whitman has nothing against society, as we have already seen, and he is always eager to embrace the new as it comes into being, but he is unwilling to characterize the new as progress, for to do so would be to admit that the world is imperfect, that it is deeply flawed, and he simply doesn't believe that. To base one's existence on the prospect of a better future denies the validity of Whitman's entire value system and enervates his refreshing emphasis on the facts of existence.

Whitman's attitude toward progress can be seen in what he says about those who purport to make the discoveries through which such advancement is supposed to come. "Hurrah for positive science," he tells us; "long live exact demonstration!" (485). And instead of undercutting what the scientist does, he exclaims "to you the first honors always!" (490). No doubt new things are discovered by scientists of every stripe—Whitman includes within this group everyone from chemists to lexicographers to surgeons and mariners—and honor ought to go to those who work for these discoveries. But in Whitman's view that which is revealed by these discoveries offers no particular evidence of progress or increasing perfection. Instead, he asserts that "Your facts are useful, and yet they are not my dwelling, / I but enter by them to an area of my dwelling" (491,92). The facts and discoveries of the scientific mind are useful only to the extent that they allow the poet a point of entry into one area of his dwelling, helping him to flesh out further one part of the larger picture to which he is devoted. Not only does this view of science diminish the scope of discovery, but it also shows that the point of all such activity is simply to know better the various areas of the human dwelling. Science points toward no utopia; it simply points insistently to that which is, helping us to understand where we live a bit better.

These sentiments are quite "un-American" for the most American of poets, but Whitman's larger aesthetic vision could not assert anything else and still maintain its fundamental ties to the world of the here and now, the tangible world that is always so easy to ignore and yet that is the most perfect of possibilities we shall ever know. At the same time, Whitman does not deny the existence of positive change; on the contrary, "Song of Myself" recognizes in any number of ways that there has been change for the better, and the poet hopes to make things better in the future through his poem. For a democratic poet who speaks the word "En Masse," Whitman obviously hopes that more democratic feelings will result from his own work. He speaks with the voice he has to prompt others to celebrate the same world he sees, and thus the poem is designed to effect change as much as to celebrate. In asserting that "Through me many long dumb voices, / Voices of the interminable generations of prisoners and slaves" (508,9) are given utterance, Whitman knows that such voices have not been heard in the past and hence positive change has allowed the silent to have something to say.

Similarly, in launching "all men and women with [him] into the unknown" (1136), Whitman is positively exhilarated by the possibilities for change even as he recognizes the impetus for such change: "The past is the push of you, me, all, precisely the same, / And what is yet untried and afterward is for you, me, all precisely the same" (1119,20). The push of the past exists precisely because it suggests things that didn't work and prompts us to imagine untried paths to make the future better. It is the push of all of us and prompts us to do the best we can to try out the untried and see what develops. Just as quickly, however, Whitman adds: "I do not know what is untried and afterward, / But I know it will in turn prove sufficient, and cannot fail" (1121,22), and again we come back to the fact that there was never any more perfection than there is now. Inevitably, that which is has always proved sufficient—has always been as perfect as it could be—and just as inevitably that which has followed after it in its turn has proved sufficient and cannot fail to do otherwise. This larger vision does not deny the value of change, or the need for it, or the crucial way in which the celebration of life itself is tied to the changes Whitman wants to effect; it simply puts conceptions of perfection and progress in their place, as secondary, relative and finally unimportant ways of measuring the value of an individual life or life in general. Life does not have value because it progresses; it has value because at every moment it is as sufficient as it could possibly be, and the striving for that sufficiency is far more important than any specious yardstick of progress or local improvement.

Whitman's vision of perfection does not, however, deny what others call imperfection. He simply deals with the "flaws" of the world in a different way. When he tells us that "I am not the poet of goodness only, I do not decline to be the poet of wickedness also" (463), he suggests that he does not find wickedness to be a mark of imperfection in the world. It does exist, and Whitman possesses evil himself, but rather than trying to deny his own wickedness, Whitman simply recognizes it as part of the overall pattern of the world. He may strive as much as others do to act on good principles, but even if he argues that in many respects humans are seemingly godlike creatures, he recognizes at the same time that they are all capable of wickedness, that such tendencies are as much a part of their nature as the good proclivities.

Whitman also has a different idea of what is truly evil and what is not, and again boldly declares that:

> Through me forbidden voices,
> Voices of sexes and lusts, voices veil'd and I remove the veil,
> Voices indecent by me clarified and transfigur'd.
>
> I do not press my fingers across my mouth,
> I keep as delicate around the bowels as around the head and heart,
> Copulation is no more rank to me than death is.
>
> I believe in the flesh and the appetites,
> Seeing, hearing, feeling, are miracles, and each part and tag of me is a miracle.
>
> Divine am I inside and out, and I make holy whatever I touch or am touch'd from,
> The scent of these arm-pits aroma finer than prayer,
> This head more than churches, bibles, and all the creeds. (516–526)

The "forbidden voices" of the world gain speech through the poet, and he is not simply talking about those who are considered unsavory by the rest of the world. On the contrary, Whitman finds the forbidden voices to be in everyone—including himself—even if they find their most obvious expression in the lives of those society has rejected. And if Whitman claims to clarify and transfigure these voices, he doesn't mean to eliminate the "voices of sexes and lusts"; he transfigures them by giving them their proper voice, by allowing them to take their essential part in the scheme of life. Others may find these voices to be expressions of human evil, but the poet argues that they could not be. After all, they too are part of the natural urges of the world, and hence they deserve expression and celebration as much as any other urges.

When we are told that Whitman keeps "as delicate around the bowels as around the head and heart," we see how willing he is to accept all of his nature. Far from acting as though he has no bodily functions, he considers them as carefully as he does matters of the head and the heart. Most may believe that it is better not to speak about such things, to keep one's finger in front of one's mouth, but for one who asserts that "Copulation is no more rank to me than death is," such urges need to be spoken of if one is to get a firm understanding of the whole of life. The senses and the bodily urges are all "miracles" to Whitman, just as "each part and tag of [him] is a miracle," so there is no reason to restrict his poem to those aspects of existence others deem appropriate. A poem must include everything if it is to render properly the marvelous nature of existence, and Whitman doesn't blush at the task.

If for many the bodily urges are evil, and if wickedness in general is often thought to be something about which nothing should be said, Whitman recognizes that to deny these aspects of living is to deny the world of which we are a part. The only way to avoid the bodily is to act as though the present world does not exist, to imagine oneself into a totally ethereal domain that is untouched by things of the senses and by the necessities of eating, excreting, copulating and the like. This denies the most fundamental aspects of our existence, however, those parts of us upon which all the others rest. So Whitman has no difficulty in asserting in the face of his bodily urges that "Divine am I inside and out, and I make holy whatever I touch or am touch'd from." He is wholly divine and godlike, from his bowels to his mind, since the one can't exist without the other and since he clearly relishes the world of the senses in any case. He finds "The scent of these arm-pits aroma finer than prayer" because his armpits ooze the smell of real life, of everyday existence in the sweaty and grimy world.

. . . . .

"Song of Myself" also regularly expresses impatience for those who adopt a more pious view of their lives. Whitman asks:

> What blurt is this about virtue and about vice?
>
> Evil propels me and reform of evil propels me, I stand indifferent,
>
> My gait is no fault-finder's or rejecter's gait,
>
> I moisten the roots of all that has grown. (464–67)

If he assumes that his poem only speaks what people have known for thousands of years, Whitman is equally aware that people do their best to avoid their knowledge and imagine the world otherwise; if he celebrates all humans and embraces us all at once, he is also not deluded into thinking that people will readily accede to what he is saying. Nevertheless, he grows weary of the pieties that cover up the world and hide humans from themselves, and at times his exasperation is such that he seems thoroughly disgusted by human existence:

> I think I could turn and live with animals, they are so placid and self-contain'd,
>
> I stand and look at them long and long.
>
> They do not sweat and whine about their condition,
>
> They do not lie awake in the dark and weep for their sins,
>
> They do not make me sick discussing their duty to God,
>
> Not one is dissatisfied, not one is demented with the mania of owning things,
>
> Not one kneels to another, nor to his kind that lived thousands of years ago,
>
> Not one is respectable or unhappy over the whole earth. (684–91)

This list of human "sins" goes right to the center of the difference between Whitman's values and the traditional ones, and it also demonstrates quite clearly that the perpetual discontent that drives most people is more "evil" for Whitman than any of the vices most humans object to. Virtue for Whitman is connected to embracing the world as it is, and the "blurt" that other people spout out of their own dissatisfaction is something with which he wants to have nothing to do.

But Whitman is no Pangloss. He doesn't see the world through artificially constructed lenses that turn evil into good and ignore everything that doesn't fit. He knows "the bitter hug of mortality" and participates in the strife of existence as much as anyone does. And in accepting everything that is, he does not at the same time live in a world devoid of choice. He *does* reinscribe our notions of what is truly good and what is not, what is valuable and what is not, and in so doing reorients us to the crucial physical aspects of our existence that we tend always to want to deny. But the choices that are made within the world are still of the utmost importance, for they are the "untried" out of which the new of the world is going to emerge, and this means that just anything won't do. The things we try, the things we choose, are based upon the push of the past, which always suggests to us those things that have worked and those that haven't, thereby providing us with an opening to try out different responses to situations. Choice is essential in this system that embraces everything because there is so much to choose from, but our possibilities are valued in terms of the past through which we have come to construe value in the things of the world. And choice is in turn framed by the limits of the "divine" selves we possess. We may be divine in some respects—as far as Whitman is concerned—but there are also limits to our divinity and to our possibilities, and Whitman is as eloquent about those as he is about everything else.

The faith in the world upon which "Song of Myself" is based can be stated very succinctly, however long it may take Whitman to work out the major permutations of it. The poetic vision is vast but precise at the same time:

> Endless unfolding of words of ages!
>
> And mine a word of the modern, the word En-Masse.
>
> A word of the faith that never balks,
>
> Here or henceforward it is all the same to me, I accept Time absolutely.
>
> It alone is without flaw, it alone rounds and completes all,
>
> That mystic baffling wonder alone completes all.
>
> I accept Reality and dare not question it,
>
> Materialism first and last imbuing. (477–84)

The two slightly different, yet centrally-linked statements here that tie the entire poem together are "I accept Time absolutely" and "I accept Reality and dare not question it." The second suggests that "Reality" is "Time," but if this is so, time itself must be the purest definition of "Materialism," that view of the world predicated on its physical nature. Time in this sense is the eternal measuring out of the physical processes of the world, and reality is simply the human perception of the way the events of the material world are measured out. This is true enough, and certainly makes perfect sense out of the other things to which the poem refers, but in order to arrive at a complete sense of what Whitman means here, we might begin by establishing what he *doesn't* mean.

When Whitman says that he accepts reality and dares not question it, he is clearly not saying that he accepts everything that is. He is only saying that he accepts everything that is *real.* Even if we grant that what he defines as real is partially dependent on his own vision of things, still we can see that for him the real is the physical, the material world of which we are a part. In contrast to this "real" reality, there is social reality, which may be based on the real but is still something else. And in accepting reality and refusing to question it, Whitman is not saying that he refuses to call into question the imperfections of the social world. Again and again he shows the ways in which the social conception of things is flawed: it denies the physical world, is based on naive notions of linearity, refuses to accede to the metaphorical smell of its own armpits, suppresses its knowledge of sex and other urges, and generally is devoted to a willed ignorance of what reality actually is. Whitman has absolutely no desire to perpetuate such deliberate obfuscation and shows repeatedly that he does not accept the social definition of what reality is. And this means that he does dare question the rules of the social game; he devotes large portions of his poem to a commentary on the ways in which the social rules are flawed and ought to be rewritten so as to be more congruent with the way the world really is.

We have seen Whitman deride those who "sweat and whine about their condition," those who are perpetually dissatisfied and those who are "demented with the mania of owning things," and these human attitudes are only some of the things the poet would like to see changed. He also speaks, for example, about the fact that "conformity goes to the fourth-remov'd" (396), and is quick to deflate the typical human desires for glory: "Have you outstript the rest? are you the President? / It is a trifle, they will more than arrive there every one, and still pass on" (431,32). There is much in the human world that needs to be changed from Whitman's perspective, and he is not the least bit hesitant to point these things out. He may embrace humanity, but he doesn't accept the need to countenance human illusions as well.

In accepting reality, Whitman only accepts the inevitable, and his continual social polemic points this out. This distinction may seem minor, but it is essential to the ethical components of the poem inasmuch as it is based on a conception of human choice that assumes that the act of valuing can best occur in a context in which one knows that which can be changed and that which cannot. One accepts what cannot be changed in order to seek to alter that which can. So when

Whitman accepts reality and refuses to question it, he is simply choosing not to waste his time asking all the typically absurd questions humans ask: *Why* must I die? *Why* is it necessary for me to eat and excrete? *Why* do I have wickedness and imperfection within me? For Whitman these are givens not to be questioned. To spend one's life worrying about them is simply to waste one's time on a pointless exercise. In order to ask the right questions, one must first learn to accept that about which nothing can be done.

It is not enough, however, to accept that which cannot be changed. The way in which one accepts the inevitable is equally important, for in a banal way we have no real choice about accepting reality. Humans can decide to ignore it, suppress their knowledge of it or displace it onto something else, but finally reality must be accepted. Whitman's acceptance of it is clearly based not on resignation but on affirmation, and only an affirmative acceptance will do. "Song of Myself" celebrates life, *all* of it, and accepts everything that is real as real rather than trying to make it into something it isn't. And while it may seem an easy task to accept affirmatively the reality of the world—and while it is inevitable in some senses that we must finally accept this reality regardless—Whitman's poem shows us that it is a difficult thing to accomplish, that indeed it is the hardest thing human beings have to do, given as they are to illusions of omnipotence and immortality. Whitman prefigures writers like Nietzsche who demonstrated how difficult yet essential it is to affirm the inevitability of reality in the face of all of the things about it that humans don't want to confront. Whitman's work, like Nietzsche's, is, after all, as much a critique of the social illusions we create to avoid accepting reality as it is an affirmation of what is, and both critiques demonstrate that the social illusions through which we live our lives are finally denials of reality rather than affirmations of it and are negative ways of living rather than positive ways of choosing within the world.

Whitman puts the difficulty and the necessity for affirming life as simply as he can phrase it when he says "I accept Time absolutely." The implications of that phrase are enough to establish the validity of the entire poem, even if it also sounds so simple as to require no further commentary. As with accepting reality, to accept time absolutely seems a foolish notion chiefly because we have no choice, but Whitman knows that the social game is based on the denial of time and all that is involved in such a rejection. To accept time absolutely is to accept without question the processes of the natural world and one's place within them, and to do this is to accept all of those things about humanity that humans have traditionally tried to reject, from the stink of the armpits to the stench of death. Virtually everything within the linear structure of society is devoted to keeping from us the knowledge of time, allowing us to defer still longer an awareness of what it means to be fully human. The ultimate measure of all our lives is time simply because it gauges where we have been, where we are, and where we will be, and its changes are written into every aspect of our existence.

To accept time means to accept the material world, and to accept it means to accede to the fact that there are certain inevitabilities about life that cannot be changed. And while it is easy enough in a way to accept all this in the first blush of youth, Whitman is 37 when he writes this line, so he has lived long enough to appreciate fully what time means for him. By that age one has a history. One has a knowledge of how one got to where one is just as one knows that there are a great many things that cannot be done over again. The past has determined the future in irretrievable ways, not to be undone by any human choice, and the road one is on clearly points to the dissolution of the body at the end. The urge within all of us in such a context is to wish to do something over, to wish back one or two choices that seemed to affect our lives in ways that were unexpected. And this occurs only if one hasn't already spent one's entire life trying to wish oneself into an atemporal world where choices have no final effects, where lives are forever and everything can be undone. As Nietzsche was to point out shortly after "Song of Myself" was written, the human desire for revenge—that great desire to deny life and affirm death instead—is based upon "man's revulsion against time and its 'It was.'" Whitman's absolute acceptance of time here is made in the spirit of that knowledge.

Humans are revulsed by time. They continually seek to deny it and imagine another world where it doesn't affect them. In turn, they are revulsed by their own human natures and wish them to be otherwise. And in time they are revulsed by their past, their "It was," for it limits their possibilities for the future and makes them seem too firmly rooted in what has already happened. The desire to begin again is strong, and society regularly contributes to the illusion that one can begin again. Likewise, the stratagems through which we seek to deny time are endless and omnipresent—it is always easy enough to wish oneself into a future that will be better, always simple to deny the present and work toward a future that will never come or a past that will never return. It is far more difficult to accept that what *is* cannot be changed, that whatever change will come will derive from what has already happened. Nietzsche knew that it was the hardest thing of all for humans to accept time—that is why he asserted that his one hope for a better human was that we would learn how to abrogate the desire for revenge—and Whitman too understands that it takes all of one's human potential to accept time absolutely, just as he knows that to do otherwise is to deny the value of life itself, to assert that, at best, the universe is "middling well as far as it goes" but hardly enough to fulfill human desire.

Whitman doesn't simply state that he absolutely accepts time, though; he also tells us that "it alone is without flaw, it alone rounds and completes all, / That mystic baffling wonder alone completes all." Presumably time is without flaw *because* it and only it rounds and completes all, because it alone allows us to have a proper measure for our lives and thereby provides us with a rounded and complete way of evaluating where we are at any particular moment. Without it value would be impossible, for there would be no reason to choose one thing over another; without it, there would be no reason to do anything; and without it there would be no way of properly gauging what has already been done and measuring the effects of what has already occurred. If one's desire is for another world, then time is hardly flawless—it is a reflection of the crucial flaw in the universe, that which dooms everything to decay and decrepitude. But if one accepts one's place in the universe, time becomes the perfect mark for the dynamics of existence and the perfect gauge of human choice in a world that is always open to the new that emerges out of the past. It is in that light that Whitman celebrates it, accepts it and declares it alone to be without flaw.

Whitman knows that he takes "no hurt from the fetid carbon" (1155) of life; he knows that being "hugg'd close" by it for a long time before he was born was as crucial to his life at the moment as anything else. He is not offended by having been built out of molecules of carbon because they are his link to every other living thing in the world, and the unfolding permutations of this molecule of life had everything to do with the preparations the world made for him. In asserting "I am an acme of things accomplish'd, and . . . an encloser of things to be" (1148), Whitman knows that the immense preparations of the world that generated him were based on carbon, and that all of its changes have led to him, the momentary acme of things already achieved. This doesn't make him special, of course, since the same can be said for every living organism at any given time, but it does give him the necessary perspective to accept his temporal existence and to place himself comfortably within it.

To accept time absolutely, however, also means that there will be no respite for us in life; time does not stop, and there is no place for us to step out of it. When Whitman exclaims "I tramp a perpetual journey" (1202), he is emphasizing that our "tramping" never ends—there is *work* involved in walking through life, all the more so because there is no haven outside of time. Whitman then very quietly tells us that "after we start we never lie by again" (1219), and even if it takes us a while to realize the full force of that statement, we eventually come to see how many human illusions of "rest" are undone at a stroke. Our metaphysical worlds, after all, were built in large part on the idea of rest, of a haven away from the cares that overtake us in everyday life. We have repeatedly imagined locations in the world outside of time precisely so we could put by the burden of living *in* time, but if we accept time absolutely, we must in turn accept the full weight of its force: there is no spot outside of it, no vacation from it.

The broad acceptance of time that "Song of Myself" declares also relates finally to our usual conceptions of fulfillment and satisfaction. We imagine a world outside of time so that we can dream of total fulfillment, a spot where no further striving on our part is required. We grow tired of the journey, after all, because we never seem to be quite satisfied with the way things are, and we wish we could be. To accept time absolutely is forever to put an end to our hopes for the paradise of pure happiness as we conjure it, and Whitman does not hesitate to tell us so. In one sense we might find it curious that he would deny fulfillment to us, for he has insisted again and again that the world is as perfect as it could be, and he has also embraced the full reality of life with such exuberance throughout the poem that we are perhaps given to thinking that he has somehow found what we lack: total satisfaction with his life. But Whitman undermines that belief as well:

> This day before dawn I ascended a hill and look'd at the crowded heaven,
>
> And I said to my spirit *When we become the enfolders of those orbs, and the pleasure and knowledge of every thing in them, shall we be fill'd and satisfied then?*
>
> And my spirit said *No, we but level that lift to pass and continue beyond.* (1220–23)

Human existence is never completely "fill'd," however much we should like it to be, and no amount of knowledge about the world can ever change that fact. We can certainly experience the pleasures of the world in all their fullness, and we can be delighted by much in our lives, but we shall never be fully satisfied. For humans this is perhaps the hardest thing to accept, and Whitman shows that it is difficult for him to accede to it as well; the very fact that he asks his "spirit" if such "filling" is ever possible demonstrates how much he too at times wishes he could believe in the eternal moment of fulfillment. He may embrace life fully, but he remains unfulfilled for all that, so he comes to see that to accept time is by no means to achieve the goal that humans have desired from the beginning. Rather, it is to put an end to the wish (for) fulfillment forever.

Finally, however, the acceptance of temporality is based on a far simpler proposition, one that is again easy to state but difficult to accept: "That which fills its period and place is equal to any" (1143). The "goal" of life in Whitman's perspective is simply to fill one's period and place, to make the best use of those things that are available to one in view of what one is, where one is and how one got there. The limitation of this is that "any thing is but a part," when we desire to be more than a part, but inasmuch as we aren't capable of being anything more than a part of the vast processes around us, we ought instead to concentrate on filling out our place within the whole as best we can. That is what Whitman seeks to do, and he is willing to live with this lesser role. He wants only to "shoulder his duds" and get to work on filling out his place within the world. And with that view he can accept both his limits and his true potential; he can live within the world as it is even as he seeks to make changes from his local vantage point; he can live with the bitter hug of mortality and still celebrate the richness of the life he finds everywhere; and he can comfort himself with his understanding of things at the same time that he realizes that in the end the mystery in the midst of which he stands remains untranslatable. It is, and that is enough.

. . . . .

Whitman's vision in "Song of Myself" is certainly comprehensive, and it fleshes out a new kind of aesthetic in a dramatic and democratic way. The poet's "barbaric yawp" is just that in many respects, but, like the sweat of his armpits, he accepts the voice that has been given him and simply tries to make the best use of it he can. The barbaric yawp of the poem, however, is not simply a result of the poet's limitations; it is part of the expression of the new aesthetic that he is developing. His aesthetic takes issue with the rarefied visions of poetry that precede (and follow) his, and it is precisely the barbarity that demonstrates the ways in which the aesthetic involves an ethic. Whitman's voice in the poem is not contrived to adapt to a different linguistic medium; it is the voice he uses in everyday life, for his aesthetic is meant to speak to the everyday world. To be sure, the form of poetry prompts Whitman to make use of that voice in different ways—he doesn't normally speak in vast catalogs, doesn't normally use the repetition of key phrases as a linking device—but the voice is still the one that Whitman carries with him wherever he goes. In choosing not to change his voice to suit the poem, Whitman also refuses to turn his poetry into a region of hidden desire and displaced wish fulfillment. He is not writing about what could be, or should be, but about that which is, and he is therefore not articulating an ideal, other world in his poetry but rather the ideal world in which we already live.

The most essential aspect of the ethic of "Song of Myself" is precisely that it is based on an aesthetic of what is, on a vision of the beauty that exists all around us and in which we participate in our everyday lives. We do not have to go elsewhere for it; it is always right here with us, and only our artificial visions of the world have prevented us from seeing this. All poems have at least an implicit ethic, and in all too many cases over the past hundred years or so it has been an ethic of denial, one that is based upon the rejection of that which is. Whitman's ethic is not merely implicit, though; it is a central part of the entire poem, for "Song of Myself" is devoted to an expression of what it means to be wholly human and how to live within the world in which we find ourselves.

In contrast, for example, we might think of a poem like "Tintern Abbey" that is also devoted to a celebration of the mystery of the world. For Wordsworth the mystery has dimmed considerably even before the age of 30; the desire to recover a former state is the strongest motive of the poem, and the rejection of the life of maturity is quite palpable throughout the work. Implicit in this scenario is the notion that poetry itself becomes a part of a momentary recovery process that might help heal us and make us better humans, but we also face the loss of our originary connection to the world. Wordsworth does his best to affirm the value of life, contrasting "sober pleasures" with "wild ecstasy," but he is at least as much trying to convince himself as the reader that maturity is preferable to youth. In the end, Wordsworth doesn't much like the world in which he lives, and even if he can blame many of his cares on society's flaws, this is a strategy through which he is able to deny the degree to which the real problem is him and his reaction to the necessary processes of aging. Far from accepting time absolutely, Wordsworth wants to reject it, and although he is not able to do so, he can use his poems to imagine a location where he is once again outside of time, oblivious to the worries that come with age.

The ethic of this poem is clearly an otherworldly one, for Wordsworth cannot be satisfied with anything less than the blissful state that can exist only in his imagination. Thus the ethic rejects this world, refuses to affirm it, or does so feebly at best, and the result is that poetry itself becomes little more than a retreat, momentary therapy to treat the wounds of time in a world that is all too alien.

Whitman finds nothing alien to himself, and this is what is so striking about his work. One is inclined to assume that he managed to write a poem like "Song of Myself" only by ignoring vast stretches of everyday life. But as soon as one returns to the text, one sees that everyday life is insistently there. One can in turn argue that such a united world might have been possible for Whitman given the time during which he lived, but for us moderns alienation is a fact of existence not to be avoided, and recovery—even momentary recovery—is the best we can hope for. But we must then remember that the poem includes discussions of fairly important human failures as well—the Civil War is in there, the account of the Alamo, and other fairly grisly examples of human fallibility appear often. We may be accustomed to thinking that no war could have been worse than World War I, or that World War II with its genocide and nuclear weapons was still worse, but in its own context surely the Civil War was as horrifying to its observers as any other, and Whitman had more than his share of caring for the wounded and dying, so he was hardly oblivious to the horrors humans were capable of perpetuating.

Nor does Whitman propose any specific solutions to the evil in the world. That is not the job of poetry. But he does provide an aesthetic whose ethic is broad enough to embrace the possibility of change and the need for dealing with that which is evil. Again and again, Whitman's ethic begins with the simple acceptance of what is, just as his aesthetic is based upon the beautiful rhythms of the everyday world in which we live. He accepts his evil not so that he may become more evil, but so that he may become less so. He proposes that only by recognizing all of his capabilities for good and ill will he be capable of acting more often on the good, though he concedes that the evil within him will never go away.

The ethic of the poem is quite simple, just as the aesthetic is: accept the nature of what is, and build the future on the basis of it. Perceive as well as possible the rhythms of life and the ways in which one is integrated into them, and then seek as much as possible to reinforce the value of those rhythms rather than fighting against them. Those two choices—really the same choice differently expressed—allow Whitman to see the world as a fully measured and beautiful place just as they provide him with the means for measuring it himself. In many respects "Song of Myself" is very much a stoical poem in that it is based upon the premise that one builds one's ethics—and one's aesthetic—on the ground of necessity, and it is precisely that strong sense of knowing what is and isn't the case that makes the poem so refreshing in the end.

The problem with this ethic and the aesthetic out of which it arises is that it denies too many of our ruses. It refuses to countenance any of our traditional ways of avoiding the truth. Whitman doesn't try to convince us that we are building up stock for a possible future life during this one—there is no such end point. He doesn't try to convince us that social success is the key to human value—he shows it to be a shallow response to the anxiety of death. Whitman does not proclaim progress or improvement of any kind and offers no "goals" for life beyond the obvious one of celebrating it as fully as one can. For us this makes the poem all too difficult to bear in some respects, for we have long since ceased being able to appreciate the value of living as a goal in itself. And we have reduced the Whitmanian vision to something totally contrary to it, a mindless kind of hedonism or a superficial sense of self-fulfillment. Whitman is only secondarily, if at all, interested in fulfilling himself, and he is the last person to exploit the senses for their own sake. He is always measuring, measuring, gauging the ways things work, the way things are, and if he uses his senses primarily to do this, he uses them as mysteries to be penetrated along with all the others in the world. As for self-fulfillment, Whitman is more interested in *world fulfillment*—he wants to launch us all into the Unknown so that we can do our best to fill out the world as is fitting. If we do that we shall surely be fulfilled ourselves, but that fulfillment comes as a consequence of a larger activity and is hardly to be sought for itself.

One can phrase the ethical question of the poem in a different way by stating that the aesthetic upon which "Song of Myself" is based is different from many other versions of beauty because it is *difficult*. To be sure, many poets go to great lengths to remind us of the difficulties they had in trying to render their revelation of the beauty of the world in words, but the vision itself came easily, and the implications of it didn't stray far from the perception. Whitman perceives the same patterns and rhythms as other poets, but his is a difficult aesthetic in conception, not simply in articulation. It is so difficult because it forces us to realize the countless illusions through which we construct our lives. It is difficult because in order to perceive it fully one must be willing to forgo those illusions. Too many poets make beauty too easy by leaving us with the impression that it is too fragile a thing for the world, but they make it too easy on themselves by doing so. They avoid all the implications of their visions by restraining them, by placing them in airtight chambers where their full richness and difficulty are not seen. We are only meant to imagine all the trouble the poet went through in order to bring us his special vision.

Here again, though, Whitman's poem speaks more accurately about the question of the aesthetic. If many poets have struggled mightily to achieve their insights into the beautiful, this is hardly heroic. They have had to struggle only because they have fought at least equally hard to hold on to their illusions about life in general, and those illusions have made the aesthetic recede further in the distance. Whitman's aesthetic requires no struggle to capture, but it demands something far more difficult: the right kind of *life*. If one has the right kind of life, then the aesthetic is always available, so it is not hard to perceive and the difficulties of expressing it are rather minor as well. But to achieve the right kind of life is the most difficult thing any human can do, so the aesthetic is not so easily available for most.

Of course, in the late twentieth century we are hesitant to speak about "the right kind of life." We think we have seen too much even to think of using such a phrase. We have been relativized so much that we actually believe at some level that all ways of life are of equal value, except in the privacy of our own homes, where we might be willing to hazard a few statements about right and wrong ways to live. We see it as a virtue that we are unwilling to speak about things like the right way to live even as we mourn the loss of meaningful values, failing to see the connection between the two things. There are many good reasons why we ought to be hesitant in proclaiming right and wrong ways to live, particularly because many of the worst people of the century had no qualms at all about asserting what was good and evil. But part of our discomfort about ideas of right and wrong ways to live has to do with a misperception about what such terms should mean, and this problem is compounded even more when one is speaking about a poem and its ethical implications. We have denuded poetry of ethical questions in part, after all, precisely because we haven't wanted to consider them anywhere else either, and the feeling that somehow such questions ought not to apply to poems is quite right if those questions are narrowly defined.

But when I speak of the difficulty of living the kind of life upon which the aesthetic of "Song of Myself" is predicated I don't mean to suggest that Whitman has any particular prescriptions about life in mind. He doesn't. Nevertheless, the poem makes a clear distinction between the right kind of life and the wrong kind, and that distinction has to do with whether or not one's existence finally affirms the value of life in its entirety. In a very loose sense, anyone who has yet to commit suicide has affirmed the value of life, but this is not the kind of affirmation Whitman demands of his readers. He insists on the most strenuous of human affirmations and reminds us of its difficulty again and again, beginning with the challenge embodied in the necessity for accepting time absolutely.

Human beings are essentially temporal creatures from beginning to end, and while we might not always notice the ways in which time affects us—or the ways in which we react to it—a careful look at a typical day would reveal the countless ways in which we are always displacing ourselves into a past that is a refuge from the present, or positing ourselves into a future that will not require a refuge. All too many of our projects are either implicitly or explicitly based on dissatisfaction with the present and a desire to set things right. And all this is to say nothing about the peculiarly American myth that we are always capable of making ourselves over anew, of starting over in life once we've made a botch of it. We elect presidents who assure us that "It's morning again in America" and lap up advertisements that regularly tell us that everything is reversible, especially the aging process itself. Such appeals work precisely because we want to believe that things can be done over if need be, that we can begin again and face the world without the burdens of what we have already become.

At the same time we all come to find that it is *not* possible to begin again. We can move, change jobs, remarry, get a facelift or do countless other things, but in the end we are forced to realize that we are stuck pretty much with what we are. We are what we are on the basis of where and when we were born, who our parents were, what events affected—and continue to affect—us as we age, what capabilities were implicit within us from the beginning, and none of these things can be eliminated. We can work against them, but we always end up having to face them again. Our past is not eradicable, even if memory itself has been weakened. We may not be able or willing to recall what has happened to us, but it resides within us all the same, in the body and everywhere else. And to accept time absolutely is to accept that none of these things can be done away with; even more, to accept time is to accept what we are in every molecule of our beings.

When one includes in what we are all the things that remain unspoken in our society, from our sexual natures to our bodily functions to our ultimate death, one has a fairly lengthy list of things that most of us spend much of our lives rejecting, and denying life in the process. Accepting all of these inevitabilities, though, is only the beginning of accepting time absolutely, for then we come around to the larger questions of purpose, no overarching goal to life, no pattern through which one can establish permanently a reason for living. We seem to think we need reasons for living, though, and so reject a view that argues living is valuable in itself, particularly when the life is employed in valuing the things of the world as best one can. We want more; we want something to assure ourselves that all the grief and woe—and the joy and delight—fit into some bigger plan. For Whitman, the only plan they fit into is the vast project of the universe, which finally doesn't offer us the solace we require. So we keep seeping into the past and the future, looking for a way to resolve all of the difficulties inherent in being ourselves.

Whitman's aesthetic, then, is more than sufficient as a description of the mysteries of the world and is rich enough to take account of all the things that need to be accounted for. But it is also dependent on the difficulty of accepting the world as it is rather than trying to mold it to our secret desires, and its value is not really discernible until one is willing to put off the illusions the social game offers us. And in one sense the ethic of the aesthetic involves nothing more than coming to this realization and acting in terms of it. Once one has accepted what one is and what the world is, then the act of valuing itself can first begin seriously to take place. Until that time, value is determined on the basis of what isn't, on what we would like to be rather than what actually exists, and as such all values deny rather than affirm our existence. The dividing line between these two states is virtually indistinguishable in everyday life, yet the mark between the two articulates a vast gulf that cannot be bridged by half solutions and temporary commitments. One finally either affirms or denies life in his choices, and one's assessment of his own life ultimately depends upon which way one chooses to live.

The ethical question of "Song of Myself" can also be phrased another way, as all questions of value can be. It is the question not only of how to choose but also of what is included and excluded as the result of one's choices. In a superficial way one can say that the poem includes everything and everyone and is quite deliberate in doing so. Whitman feels a special alliance with the outcasts of society—with the whores and the poor and the thieves—and sympathizes with the way they have been excluded. After all, the outcasts are cast out because they refuse to accept the standard illusions about goals and achievements, either by choice or necessity, and deny society's values by the life they choose to lead. Whitman himself clearly realizes the ways in which his own values undercut the rules of society and so must to a certain extent feel cast out himself. He doesn't share the conception of reality that allows one properly to succeed in the larger world.

At the same time Whitman is capable of flaunting his difference from society, emphasizing that he loafs instead of working, asserting that the smell of his armpits is better than prayer, deliberately including those whom society would like to forget about. Likewise his poetic strategies are designed to mark his difference from the effete world of "serious" poetry, both in the form he employs and in the subject matter he chooses to include, both of which seem all too raw and unpoetic to the aristocratic mentality. In recognizing those things he has in common with the outcasts of society, Whitman clearly both includes them and in a real way excludes himself from the social game as well. Given this, one would expect him to be scornful of those who play by society's rules and disdainful of those who unfairly exclude others simply because their values are different, but again he surprises us, and we are forced to remember that he also insisted on being in the game. After he demonstrates his out-of-the-game view of the world—and implicitly reveals the absurdity of society's values—he doesn't turn with venom toward those who remain within the game. Instead he asserts "I have no mockings or arguments, I witness and wait" (81). He doesn't mock those who subscribe to social reality; he simply witnesses and waits. In part he adopts this attitude because he himself has gotten too bound to the social game in the past, as we see when he tells us "Backward I see in my own days where I sweated through fog with linguists and contenders" (79). He too once assumed that the social world was reality and got lost in the fog, and to stand at a later date and deride those who are still wholly within the social mist would be to deny part of himself and to negate his own past. So instead of mocking those who remain within the comfortable inclusions of society, Whitman simply witnesses about his own vision and waits to see what happens. He is not going to reverse the game and start excluding the included simply because he knows what it feels like to be excluded and wants others to know what it feels like.

Whitman seems, then, to be all inclusive. Instead of excluding one thing or another, rejecting one group or another; instead of simply reversing society's rules; he accepts those who fall under their sway as well. This too is a common strategy of those who have felt the whip of social constraint, though by no means the only one. Far more typical is the simple reversal of values, the desire to make the master the slave and to assert one's own mastery, thereby ignoring everything one learned about the pain of slavery. Whitman's broadly inclusive choice seems more related to the kinds of feeble acceptance of everything that we see so much of today. If the "liberal" tendency is based upon the notion that everyone is entitled to his or her own values, and that therefore one ought simply to remain silent about one's own values—or even seek strenuously not to have any particular values—one might be inclined to assume that Whitman too embraces this view. But he clearly doesn't. He accepts other systems of values as necessary and inevitable and is not about to mock others for believing in things he himself has rejected, but he still witnesses for his own way of seeing the world. He doesn't remain silent about what he finds valuable—he proclaims it loudly for anyone who will listen. But if people don't want to listen, he doesn't use his values as a means through which to deny them and uphold himself. He witnesses and he waits, hoping for change but not denying the present in the mean time.

Again, the difficulty involved in Whitman's values here needs to be emphasized simply because it is too easy to assume that there is no difficulty in what he is saying. Most of us either live complacently within the social givens of our world or strenuously deny them, and both of those attitudes are far easier to adopt than the one Whitman embraces. First of all, if we remember the need to accept time absolutely, we should recognize that most of us don't accept time at all, and thus when we arrive at a point where we no longer subscribe to society's values, we want to make society pay for having imposed them upon us in the first place. We want to enslave society just as it enslaved us. The desire for revenge, the hope that the world can start anew if only we can turn the tables on the exclusionary structures of society, is so strong that most of us find it entirely appropriate to make use of the strategies we have rejected in order to impose our will on society. The alternative seems to be simply doing nothing—upholding nothing and valuing nothing—for fear that one might have to defend one's choices if they are outside of mainstream perceptions. It is most difficult to assert one's own values in a context that offers little support for them, and the tendency is either to retreat into silence or else to become demagogic and seek to impose one's values upon others.

Whitman chooses the difficult middle way: he asserts his values without imposing them on others. He waits for us, hoping that we shall find something worthy in his work, and in the meantime he continues to declare the values in which he believes. But he doesn't want to force the issue simply because he realizes that to do so would be to violate his sense of what is and thereby render his assertions valueless. He has, if you will, the patience to wait, the proper sense of temporality that allows him to assume that if his work has value, it will sooner or later be discerned. He stops somewhere waiting for us, hoping that we arrive but realizing at the same time that whether or not we do is beside the point at the moment—for now he must simply assert his values and see what happens as a result.

Whitman insists on our ability to take what he has given us and make use of it; likewise, he is very clear about his own role in our understanding: "You shall not look through my eyes either, nor take things from me, / You shall listen to all sides and filter them from yourself" (36,7). It is significant that he does not wish to impose a dogmatic vision upon us, more significant still that he sees the reader as an active participant in the process of measuring the world through "Song of Myself." What is most important in these lines, though, is that we shall "filter" the various ideas of the poem "*from*" our own selves; the "from" is one of those totally unexpected little words in the poem that demonstrates how well Whitman understands what he is doing. We as readers take in his words, but their worth is determined by the ways in which the words are filtered from us; they bring to the fore aspects of our own existence, and in so doing confirm the value of Whitman's words as a filter through which our own lives can come to clarity. In letting us see ourselves and our own values, "Song of Myself" is thus deliberately designed to prompt us to begin understanding our own modes of choice in new ways.

Even more, the return to the word "filter" at the very end of the poem establishes yet another important sense of the valuing that is at the center of "Song of Myself." Imagining the world and his effect upon it once he is gone, Whitman asserts:

> You will hardly know who I am or what I mean,
>
> But I shall be good health to you nevertheless,
>
> And filter and fibre your blood. (1341–43)

As part of the dirt in which the grass grows, Whitman and his work will filter the impurities out of our blood, making us stronger in the process. Our "good health," then, will come from the ways in which Whitman's poetry allows us to separate the useful from the meaningless, the valuable from the dross. We will be able to avoid the "infections" that come from a life of illusions.

If the ethic of "Song of Myself" is broadly inclusionary, then, it is also an ethic of choice. Whitman includes everything, but he values some things over others, yet another seeming paradox that is crucial to our understanding of the poem. The poet clearly chooses to see the world in terms of the natural rhythms that saturate it, and this choice in turn prompts him to devalue the rules of the social game, even if he still participates in it. He does not deny that there is value to social reality, only that there is less value to it than that which inheres in the natural order. It is this choice, after all, that allows Whitman to see the artificiality of social reality in the first place, and this in turn allows him to make sense out of the rhythms of his own being. Society cannot explain Walt Whitman because it denies too much of human nature and forces human activity onto a linear grid designed to produce work for specific ends. And if Whitman does perform work for society, he does so within the larger framework he establishes in the poem as a whole, placing the point of his activity in a secondary position.

The question of choice within the poem does not involve exclusions in a large sense, though it does in the narrow context. Given two choices, the poem suggests, that which more thoroughly corresponds to the aesthetic rhythms of the world is that which should be chosen. But inasmuch as one always lives in a context that includes society, such a choice cannot at the same time deny social reality. It must accommodate the pressures of the local context as well if it is to be a proper decision. Choices thus are seen always in terms of relationships, of weighing one thing over the other without denying the validity of the other, and this applies to individuals as much as it does to personal choices that have nothing in particular to do with other humans. One way or the other the world must be chosen every time one values one thing over another, and for that to happen the choice must not be based on a rigid framework that denies the possibility of change in the future.

The particulars of human choice are displayed in many ways throughout "Song of Myself," most pertinently perhaps when Whitman tells us that

> What is commonest, cheapest, nearest, easiest, is Me,
>
> Me going in for my chances, spending for vast returns,
>
> Adorning myself to bestow myself on the first that will take me,
>
> Not asking the sky to come down to my good will,
>
> Scattering it freely forever. (259–63)

Whitman seems to be suggesting a curious kind of value system here by asserting that he prefers what is "commonest, cheapest, nearest, easiest," as though he would simply choose that which caused him the least difficulty. As with the word "loafing," though, we must interpret this line in a different way. As he is clearly enamored of the grass, for example, Whitman prefers those things that are easily ignored by others in their pursuit of the glories of the social world. Like grass, the things he values are common, so common as to be disregarded almost altogether. Like grass, they are cheap in social terms precisely because they are not valued. Like grass, they are inevitably part of the local environment that surrounds Whitman. If they are the easiest choices to make for these reasons, yet it is not Whitman's fault that they are easy because so few other people truly value them.

The central factor in Whitman's value system is simply to make use of that which is available to him; he values that which he sees around him because it is worth valuing. He doesn't need to move somewhere else to find what he desires or construct an elaborate project to achieve his goals. He values what he has and makes use of it as he sees fit. Clearly the poem as a whole suggests this attitude simply because the things that are included in it are in one sense little more than bricolage—Whitman has picked up all the oddments around him that he finds valuable and has woven a poem out of them. There would doubtless have been a great many other things he could have included—some of them far more exotic or esoteric—but there was no need to travel the earth in search of material because the poet had everything he needed right in his local environment. If Whitman the bricoleur had lived in San Francisco, the materials of his poem would have been considerably different, but the value system that chose those materials would have remained the same, and inasmuch as it is the system of values itself that Whitman hopes to reveal to us, the local material could be almost anything.

Two other lines from the above passage also bear remark, though, for they frame the opposing sides of value for Whitman. He recognizes that his life is simply a case of "going in for [his] chances, spending for vast returns," and he does not ask the "sky to come down to [his] good will." In picking out the things of value, his choices involve chances—what he picks up and the way he puts it together have everything to do with how his life turns out, so there is risk involved. Whitman hopes through his choices to generate "vast returns," but the economic language should not blind us to the fact that he is primarily interested in the richness of his life—it is that richness that is at stake in his choices, and it is contingent on willingly taking his chances to see what will happen. Not only is he willing to live with what happens; he doesn't expect help from an external, otherworldly source. The sky has nothing to do with the way things work out, and its good or bad will is beside the point when it comes to the elements of life that Whitman builds out of that which is around him. He chooses and builds with his best knowledge of the rhythms of the world, but that doesn't mean that the world is looking out for his interests. The sky is indifferent to Whitman, as is the natural world as a whole, where one individual means next to nothing at all. Whitman is thus free from the constraints imposed by an external source.

It should be noted, though, that this freedom from external compulsion doesn't make Whitman the first existential hero. He does not see himself as making choices in a vacuum, solely in terms of what is good for him, and perhaps for all humanity. His choices are based on his understanding of the measure of the world, something that is outside as well as inside him, something that doesn't compel him to make this or that choice any more than it encourages one thing over another. The value of his choices is dependent only on the degree to which he is capable of perceiving the measure of the world, and the better he is at discerning that, the better his choices will be, regardless of the common and cheap things through which he builds his existence.

"I exist as I am, that is enough" (413), Whitman proclaims early on in the poem, and that, perhaps, should be enough for us too. Certainly such a statement is dependent upon a high degree of certitude about that which is valuable in the world, for it assumes that one's choices are not dependent on the need to convince others that one is indeed enough as one is. And in the end, the value of "Song of Myself" for its readers is based upon the duality inherent in its two central assertions: I exist as I am, that is enough; the world exists as it is, that is enough. Those may be two of the most difficult statements to live through, but if they are pursued, they reveal the beauty of the world from its commonest level to its grandest; they make us aware of the ways we participate in and contribute to the vast unfolding of the world; and they provide us with the essential context for valuing in our own lives on a daily basis. They do not provide the specifics for existence—we are on a knoll and not a mountaintop—and the poem would be a failure if it were to try to detail the ways in which we should live. Such things must be determined individually on the basis of an acceptance of what is. But for Whitman, there is nothing surer than the sense of value that permeates the world when it is seen from this vantage point, and for us there is nothing more valuable than seeing the ways in which this grand aesthetic articulates an equally grand ethic that is fitting to life at every level.

Chapter Two

STEVENS' CHORALE TO THE ADVENTURER IN HUMANITY

While Wallace Stevens is not always seen as a descendent of Whitman, and while there is much in Stevens' work that seems to call into question a poem like "Song of Myself," the links between the two poets are important, and one of the central connections is the understanding both arrive at about the relationship between the aesthetic and the ethical. Much of Stevens would seem to deny an ethical component to literature. Indeed, as a "high Modernist," he often seems much more interested in the self-referentiality of language than he is anything else. And when his poems do concern the relationship between the human and natural worlds, Stevens is far less confident than Whitman that we can ever really know the natural world, or that there is really anything worth knowing. Nevertheless, in poems like "The Idea of Order at Key West," "Of Modern Poetry," and especially "Esthétique du Mal," Stevens demonstrates his kinship quite clearly even as he makes some adjustments to the Whitmanian heritage.

Probably the most obvious difference between Whitman and Stevens when it comes to an understanding of the natural world is that what seems so easy for Whitman is mightily difficult for Stevens. I have argued that Whitman's casual sense of the world is based upon the most difficult of human choices, but even so he has no doubt that there is a natural world, that he is part of it, and that the common rhythms between the two generate the beauty and value in life. Stevens lives in the shadow of Modernism. He is an alienated creature, doubting himself and nature, doubting even more the poet's ability to make sense of whatever relationship there is between the two. Thus, his work seems much more a quest to recover what Whitman always had about him, and his sense of the value of things is determined in part by his need to struggle for what came so easily to Whitman. In one sense, this makes

Stevens' work the more heroic, for he seemed not to be suited by temperament for the vision Whitman articulated, and it is all too easy to assume on the basis of Stevens' poems that he never left his own mind and never believed he could, even if he might have hoped that that was possible. His temperament was certainly not open and "indiscriminate" like Whitman's, and yet, I shall argue, in spite of the difficulties his own disposition put in the way, he ended up affirming virtually the same world view that Whitman celebrated, albeit in his own particular way.

If we look at Stevens' relatively early work, we are at first hard pressed to find the connection to Whitman. A fresh reading of "The Idea of Order at Key West" seems to undermine any connection there might be between the two poets, first because the poem is more about poetry than the world—or at least seems to be—and second because what it has to say about the natural world seems to undercut Whitman's views. When we are told that "She sang beyond the genius of the sea, / The water never formed to mind or voice,"[1] we are to assume that whatever her song is about, it doesn't encapsulate the meaning, or even necessarily the rhythms, of the sea. The water does not form "to mind or voice," and she sings "beyond the genius of the sea," so it is safe to assume that her song is not capturing the essence of nature at all. She does not mold it, and it seems that it does not mold her either.

The sea does have a "mimic motion" that "caused constantly a cry," but the speaker tells us that it "was not ours although we understood, / Inhuman, of the veritable ocean" (i). There is alienation and separation here, for whatever inhuman sound the sea might generate, it is different from human sounds and thus cannot be encapsulated in a poem. There may be a relation between the song and the sea, but whatever it is, it evokes a gulf between the human and natural worlds rather than suggesting consonance, and the relation itself is far more mysterious and oblique than the one Whitman articulated. The sea, after all, is "Like a body wholly body, fluttering its empty sleeves": there is no mind at work in nature, so whatever sense it has is by definition an inhuman sense, and Stevens is more interested in pointing out the difference between humans and nature than he is in marking their confluence.

For Stevens language itself has become problematic, and instead of uniting humans and nature, it now marks their difference:

> The song and water were not medleyed sound
> Even if what she sang was what she heard,
> Since what she sang was uttered word by word. (ii)

The woman may think that she is singing the rhythms of the sea, expressing their force and power through her voice, but even if she "sang . . . what she heard" the song and water are not medleyed simply because "what she sang was uttered word by word." The intrusion of meaningful sounds into the scene demonstrates the difference between her song and the sounds of the water and confirms that the human world is separate from the natural one, even if individuals like the singer—and Whitman—think they are expressing the essence of nature in their poetry. In the end, those who listen to the song conclude that "it was she and not the sea we heard," admitting that if the woman intended to speak words of the sea, she has failed.

Throughout the poem we find the contrast between the woman's ordered words and the "meaningless plungings" of the sea to be the focal point, and for the most part Stevens suggests that the best that could be said of the relation between sea and song would be to admit that the sea "Was merely a place by which she walked to sing" (iii). This means that her song would be different if she were singing by the Rocky Mountains, and, given the title's emphasis, we assume it would be different if she were singing by the sea in New York, but location is about all the direction the sea seems to give. The woman would express herself differently if she were measuring her voice from a different location, because location affects the way we perceive the world, but the "world" outside of our perception of it always escapes the words that seek to encapsulate it. In this way, the natural world as a useful concept seems to have disappeared altogether, for if we cannot speak meaningfully about it through language, then we cannot speak meaningfully about it at all. It simply exists, and since we always apply meaning to anything that exists, the world in and of itself lies beyond our comprehension.

As always with Stevens, though, there is a complication to this unsatisfying relationship, expressed here by a question that insistently comes back to the two observers of the song:

> Whose spirit is this? we said, because we knew
>
> It was the spirit that we sought and knew
>
> That we should ask this often as she sang. (iii)

If the song had been able to capture the sense of the sea, it would have been totally meaningless to the observers, just as if it were the "outer voice of sky"; it would have been nothing more than "The heaving speech of air, a summer sound / Repeated in a summer without end / And sound alone" (iv). As such, the song would be meaningless rather than meaningful; it would do no more than suggest the utter senselessness of the sea's sounds and would thereby have confirmed our total alienation from the sea.

We knew from the beginning of the poem, however, that the woman's song didn't express the meaning of the sea. What comes forth more insistently as the poem progresses is that her song is more than she thinks it is and more than the observers can understand. Whatever her song is, it is "more even than her voice, and ours, among / The meaningless plungings of water and the wind." The woman may be "the maker of the song she sang," but her song is more than a personal vision of reality, a solipsistic expression of what things mean to her, and it is that "more" that interests the speaker. If it were only her personal expression, then it would mean nothing to the speaker and Ramon Fernandez, and they clearly derive something from it. So the song is not pure subjectivity any more than it is an objective expression of the sea's meaning. But if it is neither of those two things, what is it?

Stevens doesn't ask "What is it?" though; he says "Whose spirit is this?," a question that is far more problematic for two reasons. First, it places the significance of the song beyond the singer herself—whatever she is doing, whatever she *thinks* she is doing, she is doing something both more and less than she thinks. More importantly, the word "spirit" obviously brings the religious world into the equation, but in a way that doesn't seem to make sense. After all, the poem assumes that the natural world is nothing more than the equivalent of "meaningless plungings" throughout. There is no great metaphysical truth underlying the processes of nature that we can fathom by listening to the sea or anything else. We are in the presence of a wholly secularized world, one without metaphysical significance. And yet the insistent question of the speaker is "Whose spirit is this?" He emphasizes that "It was the spirit that we sought" and tells us in effect that that is the crucial question the woman's song raises.

The question of the "spirit" of the song places the words into another context. Having dispensed with the two most obvious possibilities—that the song is either a subjective or objective expression—the more likely alternative in a secularized world would have been to make the song an intersubjective expression. Words are, after all, a social medium, and so it would only be logical to reduce the sense of the woman's words to some communal, yet entirely social, significance. She thinks she is expressing the true essence of the sea, yet the sea escapes her song; therefore what she is really expressing is some socially derived meaning of the sea, some fictitious, artificial meaning that depends more on the needs of social life than on any meaning the sea itself might have. But Stevens undercuts this more likely description of the song by raising the question of spirit in a world devoid of spiritual meaning, and the reader is left to wonder why the poem makes this deliberate shift in emphasis.

Having established the question of the spirit of the song as the most important issue, Stevens seems to back away from it as soon as it is raised as a problem. We are told that "It was her voice that made / The sky acutest at its vanishing" (v), and that "She was the single artificer of the world / In which she sang," which suggests again a kind of subjective response to the world. We are perhaps to praise her for her artifice and to recognize the genius that allows her song to mark out the border between sea and sky—something not normally visible to us—but the emphasis on human making again seems to reduce her achievement to desire and nothing more. She *wants* the world to mean something for her, and she *makes* it mean something to her through her song. She has artificialized the sea and made it something it isn't, but then that is what humans do to things with no meaning:

> And when she sang, the sea
>
> Whatever self it had, became the self
>
> That was her song, for she was the maker. (v)

But surely the sea no more has a "self" than a stone does, so in conferring a self upon it, and in making that self her song, she has stripped the natural world of its otherness and made it human. This may be justifiable, and even inevitable given the human tendency to find meaning where none exists, but the sea itself has obviously long since left her song behind.

The speaker in turn concludes from her song "that there never was a world for her / Except the one she sang and, singing, made." But what happened to the spirit of the song? Here we find little more than an expression of the existential notion that we all make our own realities, that we are all makers who craft the world in which we live and thereby remove ourselves from the natural one into which we were born, assuming that the natural world is nothing more than a fiction we create in order to imagine a world that exists outside of the one we ourselves have created. The spirit seems to have disappeared, unless we are to look for it simply in the woman's ability to make her own world and in some way to convey it to others, even if the song expresses a world that is not the speaker's or Ramon's. We may be able to marvel at the human ability to construct private worlds, but this creates a different sense for the act of creation than the word "spirit" evokes. Yet the speaker has told us that the question of spirit would be asked often as the woman's song continued, and we have to wonder what happened to that question.

When the song ends and the speaker and Ramon start back to town, the effect of the woman's efforts seems to have changed the way the two perceive the world—it has indeed transformed their vision, if only momentarily, and while this seems to have little to do with the question of spirit, that question still resides in what the speaker asks Ramon about the changes in the perspective:

> Ramon Fernandez, tell me, if you know
> Why, when the singing ended and we turned
> Toward the town, tell why the glassy lights,
> The lights in the fishing boats at anchor there,
> As the night descended, tilting in the air,
> Mastered the night and portioned out the sea,
> Fixing emblazoned zones and fiery poles,
> Arranging, deepening, enchanting night. (vi)

Clearly the woman's song has given the two a different measure for the world, one that allows them to perceive the ways in which human order adds to the scene. Instead of seeing the glassy lights in pragmatic terms—they allow the fisherman to get to their boats in safety—the two now notice the ways in which the lights transform the landscape. They take a dark, undifferentiated space and "master" it and "[portion] out the sea," bringing order to a location that was previously without it.

As the speaker and Ramon see things, though, it is not merely a question of the human imposition of order on the natural world. After all, the sea itself has hardly changed. The mastery that the lights provide does allow different activities to take place that would otherwise be impossible, but the sea remains the sea. Likewise, the lights may in one sense portion out the sea, imposing a kind of order upon it that is totally human and artificial, but it remains unchanged for all that. The mastery of the lights is inherent in the fact that they allow *humans* to see the sea in new and different ways, but even if this order is humanly imposed, it still relates to the sea itself and is thus not unreal. The perception of the sea has been changed and offers new possibilities, and the sea is perceived through the changed order, but it is indeed a part of that order.

Equally important is the fact that the new order here is an aesthetic one, composed of "emblazoned zones and fiery poles," suggesting dimly that first Promethean act of creativity. The sea is ablaze with the marks of the lights, and the fiery poles are beautiful in their own right. In "Arranging, deepening, enchanting night," the poles manage to bring into the foreground a richer sense of the order previously lying hidden in the darkness. By marking some areas with light, the poles arrange the space and give to it a third dimension, thereby deepening the contours of space and revealing more of its possibilities. The result is that the speaker and Ramon are enchanted, are carried out of their normal perception of the world and offered a privileged view of beauty and order that would normally have been missed.

Of course, the woman's song performed the same function during the daylight hours. In marking out the point where the sky vanished, it brought a new sense of depth to the scene. Normally sea and sky blend into one two-dimensional hue at their gathering, but through the song the space is opened up and made richer. The effects of the song are not as obvious during the day as the lights' contrast with the dark is, but the aesthetic principles remain the same. Just as obviously, the aesthetic principles have been derived from the song—otherwise the speaker could not have applied them to the night landscape as the opportunity presented itself.

But the question of spirit still remains. The word "enchanting" bears the mark of spirit in the lines of this stanza, but the question is not foregrounded the way it was earlier in the poem, and we still remain uncertain about the specific relationship between human order and the natural world. Inasmuch as the aesthetic order itself is transferrable from the woman to the speaker, it is not solely a private vision, and yet it is just as clearly not a natural order either, for the sea remains essentially unchanged by the fiery lights, and the order they provide is not intrinsic to the sea itself. The spaces it marks out are not written into the sea but imposed on it, and even if they do reveal aspects of it that could not be seen without the lights, still the sea has not changed at all. The night has become enchanted, which may suggest a larger order in the light of the poles, but we still don't know whose spirit pervades the aesthetic vision.

In the end, we never arrive at an answer to the question of spirit. As with Whitman, who asserted the mystery of himself and the universe, so Stevens also embraces the final mysteriousness of the whole process. It is precisely that mysteriousness that is meant to be conveyed by the question of spirit, by the assertion of enchantment: whatever order is perceived is neither totally human nor completely natural but something that remains elusively beyond our normal categories of perception. This point is brought home most strongly in the enchanted exclamation of the speaker in the last stanza of the poem:

> Oh! Blessed rage for order, pale Ramon,
> The maker's rage to order words of the sea,
> Words of the fragrant portals, dimly-starred,
> And of ourselves and of our origins,
> In ghostlier demarcations, keener sounds. (vii)

The key words in these lines are, of course, "Blessed rage for order," and while they are a marvelous encapsulation of the urge underlying the woman's song and the speaker's perception of the night scene, they also carry further the mystery of this ordering process, and they do so in several ways. Initially, the three key words don't belong together in the conventional human order. 'Blessed" partakes of the religious domain, "rage" most often is used in the context of irrational anger, and "order" belongs with the logical, rational parts of our being. If nothing else, the line makes clear that whatever logical and reasonable traits we have, they remain driven by the "blessed rage" that compels us to order the world.

More importantly, though, these words demonstrate the unfathomable nature of the human desire for order. In using "Blessed," Stevens shows that this desire partakes of the religious even in a secularized world. It is the origin of whatever divinity we have, and it does confer value on everything we see, just as it is the primary means through which we derive and perceive the joyfulness of the world. Even if the metaphysical world has departed, that which generated it in the first place—the blessed rage for order—still remains blessed. We may have denied the space from which the world came, but we can't deny its force, and Stevens has no intention of doing so. But he does enrich our sense of the blessed by stating that what is blessed is our rage for order, and the rage seems to come from the more instinctual elements of human nature, those irrational outbursts of rage that derive from the midbrain and explode out of us without any forewarning. Stevens is not suggesting that this blessed rage is nothing more than irrational anger, but he is arguing that our blessed rage comes from the same location as that more negative reaction to the world. In the case of the aesthetic, the blessed rage manifests itself as a seemingly divine perception of the beauty and order of the world, but that perception is dependent on—and originates from—the same source as our irrational anger.

"Blessed rage for order" is Stevens' phrase for what in the old days was called poetic inspiration, and while Stevens doesn't believe that some divine voice inhabits the poet while he chants his lines, he does show that the force is the same, and it is just as beyond human control as was the original divine inspiration. It overtakes the person so inspired as much as the Muse used to inhabit the being of the poet while he was singing, and while we may not believe in muses anymore, the process of the blessed rage for order is as mysterious today as it was thousands of years ago. When the speaker asks early on "Whose spirit is this?," he is inquiring about the origin of the blessed rage for order that generates the woman's song and changes the speaker's perception of the sea as well, and if he doesn't know the answer to the question, he does not deny its value or attempt to ignore the fact that extraordinary forces are involved in our will to make.

"Rage," carrying as it does the echoes of the instinctual and primitive, connects the human desire for order to the world of the other creatures on the planet just as "Blessed" connects it to our mental abilities, and the ultimate effect of the phrase as a whole is to demonstrate that the order that emanates from the song of poetry is not simply a human fiction built out of the narrow desire for control and safety—it has that written into it, but it also has much more, and if Stevens doesn't boldly declare this rage for order to be a natural phenomenon, he comes close to doing so. The blessed rage for order is our link to—and our difference from—that which we call the natural world, and because of this the woman's song must necessarily speak of more than her own desire just as it must sing "beyond" the genius of the sea. It partakes of both, yet is somehow more and less than both as well.

The one thing the woman's song finally isn't is a purely subjective expression of desire, a localized attempt to impose order on the world and gain control. The urge underlying the song is more complex than that, and it is precisely because it is different that it is capable of expressing "Words of the fragrant portals, dimly-starred." It provides an opening—and an openness—to the world that would otherwise be impossible, but the opening remains dimly-starred—it is never clarified for us to our satisfaction and never will be. But the song reveals the words "of ourselves and of our origins" that speak of something far more profound than the simple desire to fabricate a world. They speak to the origin of the human fire—the human rage for order—that both makes and perceives at the same time, revealing "In ghostlier demarcations, keener sounds" the essence of what we and the world are. The demarcations are always ghostlier because the more we pursue origins the further they recede, but they are at least marked, and marked with keener and keener sounds.

"The Idea of Order at Key West" might be a poem about the nature of poetry, then, but it is also about much more than that, and the aesthetic vision it elaborates extends well beyond the power of poetry to embrace the blessed rage for order in all of its human manifestations. Stevens uses the device of song and poetry to pursue the nature of human ordering processes, but he does not confine himself to questions of poetry. On the contrary, like Whitman, he is primarily intent on celebrating the world and the human ability to perceive it in such a joyful way, and it is within that celebration that the ethical components of the poem find their place. Stevens has not restricted the power of the poem to a drawing-room encounter with the pleasing sounds of words; he has seen it instead as a manifestation of the force within humans that allows them to perceive the world in aesthetic ways, transforming their own sense of reality at the same time that they participate more fully within it. The poetic vision has value only to the extent that it is applied to the world as a whole, as the speaker and Ramon do when they return at nightfall, and only to the extent that it reveals something about our own natures and the world in which they finds themselves.

Nevertheless, "The Idea of Order" is not explicitly concerned with conceptions of the good and the ways in which aesthetic vision generates an appropriate system of human valuation. These things are implicit in the poem, and the implications of the "Blessed rage for order" clearly have everything to do with questions of choice and value, but Stevens does not pursue these issues at great length here. For the moment it is necessary only to keep in mind that the poem is hardly a rarefied, exclusionary vision that denies the existence of the natural world or of anything outside the human psyche. It establishes a link between us and the world and celebrates it with as much zeal as Whitman does, and its precise way of accounting for our desire for order has built into it the larger ethical questions that will appear with greater prominence in Stevens' later work.

Much the same thing could be said about a poem like "Of Modern Poetry." It seems to have little to do with ethical concerns on the surface, yet underneath it has everything to do with them and manages to elaborate on their implications more fully than "Idea of Order" does. When the poem begins with the fragmentary statement about "The poem of the mind in the act of finding what will suffice,"[2] we are immediately prompted to ask what the mind might find sufficient. Does the poem seek to articulate a fitting sense of what the world is, or is it merely concerned with momentarily satisfying the mind's ceaseless questioning? Inasmuch as Stevens tells us in a later poem that "The mind is never satisfied, never," we might assume that the poem does both: it momentarily satisfies the mind by offering a sufficient articulation of the way things are. Even so, in the modern era, such sufficiency, like the fragmentary opening of the poem, can always only be partial and incomplete.

It is also important, though, that what is sufficient is the criterion for a poem. No longer can it be assumed that any human articulation of the world will be any more than sufficient; it will suffice, perhaps, but it won't be quite what we wanted it to be, for the older images of a completed universe and a completed poem are out of place in a world that has denied totalized visions of things. On the one hand, this means that our desire is never brought to an end either; on the other, it means that the poet is always seeking a more sufficient vision. The poem is enough, yet not enough. It is complete yet incomplete, so the mind must always start over again.

Stevens uses the question of sufficiency as a contrast to the older vision that has been displaced by Modernism. He tells us that "It [the poem] has not always had / to find," that "the scene was set; it repeated what / Was in the script." The assumption here is that previous eras didn't need to question the sufficiency of their metaphysic—it was a given out of which they worked and upon which they depended. Likewise, it follows that the rules of poetry were pre-established, and the poem had only to work comfortably within them. In fact there is less truth to this than Stevens would like to have us think, but these lines do establish one important difference: in Stevens' mind the poet is required to rebuild the world, and implicitly to rebuild it every time he writes a poem. No comfortable stasis exists in this scene, and none is expected. In this context, it is true that Modern poets have a different task than earlier writers.

The particulars of the poem's sufficiency are established rather quickly in the next section of the poem, but each of the things mentioned serves to establish the needs the poem fills:

> It has to be living, to learn the speech of the place.
>
> It has to face the men of the time and to meet

> The women of the time. It has to think about war
>
> And it has to find what will suffice.

If the poem needs to be living, and if it needs to learn the speech of the place, it must both respond to the local context of which it is a part and also reflect the patterns of life itself. It is not sufficient for it simply to reflect the language of the time, though that is necessary; it must also reflect the life that exists at *all* times, and thus must participate in those patterns. In "facing" the men of the time and "meeting" the women of the time, it addresses their needs in their language, but that which it faces is finally that which all humans have always confronted. And in telling us that the poem has to "think about war," Stevens includes the larger socio-political elements of existence as well—the poem must deal with the facts of existence in the speech of its own time.

On the surface, these lines simply suggest the typical explanation of the nature of poetry: it must be both universal and particular. It must use the language of its own period yet somehow reflect the universally human aspects of existence. For our purposes, though, this is less important than the fact that Stevens has made a point of explaining that the poem must deal with the elements of everyday life. It has to face the people who are alive and address the problems of their existence. It has to think about war because war is an omnipresent aspect of human life, and it cannot be ignored simply because poetry exists in a different domain. On the contrary, poetry is part of the same world that war is, and if the poem is to be sufficient, it must address these problems in the human world. Stevens' poetry often seems to move as far away from everyday life as possible, but clearly in his own mind he saw his work as addressing the problems of being human in the twentieth century, and just as clearly he did not imagine his poetry as existing in a separate space away from these problems. If it is to be sufficient, it must be part of the same world, and if it is all too easy to assume that this poem is about the need to construct a new poetic idiom in new forms, Stevens demonstrates that the project of building new poetic forms is based not on a sterile contemplation of past poetic forms so much as on the present needs of everyday life. Poetry emanates from the world we live in, not simply from previous poems, and the context that nurtures it is precisely the everyday world that we all face.

In saying that the poem of the act of the mind must "construct a new stage," then, Stevens is not talking about poetic revolutions, though they are implicit in the statement. He is talking about the vast modern project of building a new conception of the world, of redefining the place humans have on the planet and the ways in which they interact with the things about them. This is no mere platform of technique; it derives from the need to articulate a new vision of the world. And its sufficiency is based on its ability adequately to reflect the people of the world out of which it is written, no more, no less. The stage metaphor suggests the "artificiality" of that which the poem constructs—that is, it is somehow "unreal"—but the artificiality of the poem only has to do with the fact that it is based on human forms. It must still reflect the world, even if it is an artificial construct. It must still articulate the patterns of living, even if it is composed only of words.

The sense of sufficiency a poem must achieve is based on its finite means—words belong to the human world and not the natural one—but the natural world must still somehow be articulated via the artificial sounds. Its sufficiency is to be found in the way the mind responds to its construction:

> It has to be on that stage
> And, like an insatiable actor, slowly and
> With meditation, speak words that in the ear,
> In the delicatest ear of the mind, repeat,
> Exactly, that which it wants to hear, at the sound
> Of which, an invisible audience listens,
> Not to the play, but to itself, expressed
> In an emotion as of two people, as of two
> Emotions becoming one.

The poem must be like an insatiable actor, one whose desire is only fulfilled in the moment of articulation, and like an actor, it must speak words that "repeat, / Exactly, that which [the mind] wants to hear." As with the first line of the poem, here we find the question of what the mind *wants* to hear: does it simply want to be momentarily deluded, or does it want to hear what it knows to be true? But there is no ambiguity here, for if delusion were sufficient, it would not have to be repeated exactly; a simulacrum would do as well as anything else. The "delicatest ear of the mind," however, wants to hear *exactly* that which is and will not be satisfied with less.

Nevertheless, the poem only "repeats"; the mind already knows what it wants to hear because it has already heard it—because what it hears is from the beginning an essential aspect of the mind—and the poem thus doesn't give it something of which it is unaware. It knows what is but wants to hear it articulated because it is so easily lost in the everyday world, and when it hears it, it knows that it is true. The mind in this metaphor has become an "invisible audience" that "listens, / Not to the play, but to itself." The poem speaks exactly what the mind wants to hear because it is capable of expressing the mind, articulating it fully, giving it back to the auditor in the state in which he prefers it. But the "itself" of the mind that hears the poem is not the subjective, everyday self. If it were, any poem would be incapable of expressing exactly that which it wants to hear and would not therefore allow the audience to listen to itself. The self rendered here is a fuller one, one that exists in the world, and exists in an aesthetic way rather than a subjective one. Adding another metaphor to the mix, Stevens explains that the invisible audience of the mind hears itself "expressed / In an emotion as of two people, as of two / Emotions becoming one." Whether the example be two people or two emotions, the main point is simply that two things are momentarily joined together and the normal sense of self disappears, to be replaced by an aesthetic one that allows a kind of communal rhythm to occur.

The metaphorical pattern and the "as's" in these lines, of course, give and take away at the same time, suggesting at once the kind of experience the poem is supposed to generate while also implying that the poet knows as well that language itself can only speak of such things in rhetorical, hence artificial, ways. At this point in the poem, we cannot determine the degree to which the poet himself is convinced of the veracity of the poetic experience, or the degree to which the experience itself has anything at all to do with everyday life. Inasmuch as the poem must face the people of the time and address issues such as war, we assume that the mind is satisfied with the poem not simply because it brings a moment of comfort into a life of turmoil—allowing it to see itself at its best for a brief time before it returns to the more pressing concerns of life—but also because it provides the means whereby the individual can address his life in a more meaningful way. But at the same time the poem has gone so far into the "delicatest ear of the mind" that one wonders about the larger validity of the experience.

The import of the poem is finally clarified in a return to the actor on stage, who, we are told, is

> A metaphysician in the dark, twanging
> An instrument, twanging a wiry string that gives

> Sounds passing through sudden rightnesses, wholly
>
> Containing the mind, below which it cannot descend,
>
> Beyond which it has no will to rise.

The metaphysician sits in the dark, not knowing exactly what his metaphysic is, yet he is able to articulate it through his instrument. "Twanging" is hardly the most euphonious of words, suggesting rather less than the music of the spheres, but the twanging does generate "Sounds passing through sudden rightnesses," so the aesthetic vision of what is definitely appears. It comes suddenly and is not the result of any one string. Instead, the sounds the wiry instrument give off pass *through* these rightnesses in a way that the actor himself cannot control. He plays the instrument, but he cannot determine when the sudden rightnesses will come through; he simply hopes that his twanging will in some way produce them.

The larger question, though, is what these "sudden rightnesses" are. What is "right" about them? First off, they are part of a process, for they are only perceived as the sounds pass *through* them—the rightnesses are not static but reflect the aesthetic rhythms of the world as a whole. They are right, then, because they articulate the measure that unites humans and the world of which they are a part. Their sense of rightness comes from the way in which they totally inhabit the mind, as we are told when the poet emphasizes that they "wholly / [contain] the mind, below which it cannot descend, / Beyond which it has no will to rise." Once again Stevens phrases the matter in terms of the mind: it is fully satisfied for the moment. It is wholly contained, and there is nothing more fundamental than the state it is in—it "cannot descend" any lower. At the same time, "it has no will to rise" beyond the present state it is in, so for the moment the mind is indeed satisfied. Everything is perfectly fitting for it, everything is encompassed by the sudden rightnesses through which it is passing, rightnesses that, again, "contain" the mind—it has not absorbed the world but has instead been absorbed by it.

The "sudden rightnesses" of the poem generate more than a momentary sense of fulfillment, though; they are the rightnesses through which right is determined by the individual. These rightnesses—these reflections of the way the world is and the way the human fits into it—provide the reader with an ethical sense of what is right and fitting in the everyday world too, and that is not the least of their virtues. By showing us what is fitting in the world, the poem allows us to consider our actions in terms of their fit; we are prompted to choose on the basis of making our values correspond to the rightnesses we have perceived, and thus our lives have been made better as well.

The value of poetry, then, resides in its ability to articulate for us the sudden rightnesses that are part of the larger rhythms of the world. In our everyday lives we are caught up in objective or subjective patterns that are not connected intrinsically to the larger aesthetic rhythms of the world, and without an understanding of the sudden rightnesses that poems present to us we would have no way of discerning that which was and was not fitting. And because the everyday world is lacking this sense of what is fitting in the larger framework, it depends on poems—among other things—to provide the patterns through which choices should be made. Without the aesthetic vision, we have no way of understanding those moments when the mind is satisfied and no way of applying the sense of those moments to other aspects of our lives. Without the aesthetic vision, we have no way of viewing the world in a context that reflects the larger values of the universe as a whole. Stevens is not about to call that larger vision a "natural" one because he knows that the word is fraught with all kinds of ambiguities and tends to be defined in social terms in any case. But the sudden rightnesses through which his poetry knowingly passes are based on and grow out of what Whitman would have called the natural world, the only context through which humans can finally decide the question of what is and is not fitting.

Having established the vision of sudden rightnesses, Stevens is not content to leave the poem with the metaphysician in the dark, for that would suggest that there is no applicability of these rightnesses to the world as a whole. He must return to the particulars out of which a poem is generated and speak of their necessity once more in order to make the connection between the aesthetic vision and the everyday world. The poem, he tells us, must

> Be the finding of a satisfaction, and may
>
> Be of a man skating, a woman dancing, a woman
>
> Combing her hair. The poem of the act of the mind.

We have already seen how the poem *must* be the finding of a satisfaction: the sudden rightnesses *wholly* contain the mind, so if they are present, the poem allows the reader to find momentary satisfaction. *How* the poem finds such a satisfaction, though, is based on only one necessity: it must be built out of the particulars of everyday life. These particulars must be capable of manifesting the aesthetic vision, but they can be as banal as "a woman / combing her hair" or as obviously aesthetic as "a woman dancing" or something that falls in between, as in a sport like skating that always potentially involves the sudden rightnesses of dancing. Combing, dancing and skating are all everyday activities, but they are also activities based on *rhythm,* so the subject matter of the poem must relate to our ordinary lives at the same time that it shows the ways in which the rhythms of our daily activities are informed by the sudden rightnesses that articulate a sense of what is fitting. The particulars of the poem, then, must be capable of demonstrating the rhythms of the world, but beyond that their only criterion is that they be part of everyday existence, for only then will the poem show us how these rhythms apply to our lives, and only then will we be able to see ways to make our lives more fitting in the future.

Poets have been concerned about the relationship between the "local" and the "universal" for a long time, and even if the best of poets have always insisted that the local *is* the universal, no poet does a better job of explaining why this is so than Stevens. One could argue that the particulars of a poem allow the reader to "relate" to the larger rhythms in the work, that they "ground" the reader's understanding, but that is too facile a response. One could go one step further, as Stevens does here, and argue that the particulars allow the people of the time to be "faced" and to face the issues of their own world, and this brings in the ethical component of poetry, but it is still not a sufficient explanation, if for no other reason than it fails to account for the poem's value once it is called upon to face another generation with a different context.

Stevens goes one step further by showing in "Of Modern Poetry" that the particulars disclose the ways in which the aesthetic vision is integrated into everyday life, thereby allowing us to choose on the basis of a perspective that is not readily visible in our typical conceptions of things. The particulars of a poem are always manifestations of a localized vision of the value of the world; they are assertions of that which carries weight with the writer and his culture and thus establish a specific attitude toward that which is. But if they reflect the values of the ordinary world of which the poet is always a part, they also display the recurrent human situations that generate the ethic of a place and thus reflect the act of valuing itself. This dual orientation allows Stevens to affirm the centrality of the ethical aspects of the aesthetic vision even as he demonstrates the reasons why the local is the universal.

. . . . . .

In briefly discussing "The Idea of Order at Key West" and "Of Modern Poetry," I have deliberately chosen two of Stevens' poems that do not seem readily to reflect an aesthetic with clear ethical dimensions to it. These poems are, after all, among the great Modern icons that attest to the endless self-referentiality of all poems. Both are poems *about* poems, and both could theoretically be read as little more than expressions of delight at the wonder of poetry. If these poems can be read in this way, though, there are others that more forcefully suggest that Stevens didn't see his own work in this way. Most prominent among these is "Esthétique du Mal," a poem that is striking in several ways.

"Esthétique du Mal" provides one of the few Modern articulations of the nature of evil, and it would have value for that reason alone. Its true distinction, though, is that it connects this discussion to the aesthetic, and in particular the sublime. Stevens' aesthetics of evil, or the "bad," is based on the assumption that the fear inherent in the sublime is a reflection of its connection to the "mal" of the world—we like to be lifted out of ourselves into ecstatic sublimity, but such an experience also reminds us of those things about which we'd like to forget: our smallness, our fragility, the world's indifference to our presence or absence. Stevens, of course, devoted most of his poetry to the old duality between self and other, and "Esthétique" is no different in this respect. In contrast to much of his other work, though, this poem makes a point of demonstrating the value of the otherness of the world.

Initially, the most important feature of the poem is the way it juxtaposes the sublime to the everyday. We are told that "He was at Naples writing letters home / And, between his letters, reading paragraphs / on the sublime."[3] The ordinary act of writing letters home, filled, no doubt, with accounts of the sights of Naples, is placed in the midst of the man's reading on the sublime. Just as the man moves between his location at the foot of Vesuvius and his thoughts of home, so too does he move between contemplation of the sublime and accounts of everyday life. This awkward juxtaposition is reinforced in the second stanza of this section when Stevens blithely asserts: "It was almost time for lunch. Pain is human. / There were roses in the cool café." Because the ordinary statements about lunch and the roses in the café are separated by "Pain is human," we immediately assume that each statement has the same value: the thought that it is almost time for lunch is no more or less important that the notion that pain is human. In one sense, this levels the values of the sentences, making "pain is human" no more significant than the thought that lunch is about to arrive. But we are also led to consider the import of "Pain is human" precisely because it seems out of place in the context of the ordinary. So Stevens has revealed the banality of pain at the same time that he has shown it to be a part of the everyday. Conceptually, he has likewise shown that pain is as much a part of the world as is lunch or roses in a cool café.

In this way the man reveals that his contemplation of Vesuvius—and his reading about the sublime—have had their effect. His situation demonstrates the location and importance of the sublime just as it explains the human fascination with it:

> Vesuvius had groaned
> For a month. It was pleasant to be sitting there,
> While the sultriest fulgurations, flickering,
> Cast corners in the glass. He could describe
> The terror of the sound because the sound
> Was ancient.

The volcano has been groaning for a month, conjuring up images of what happened to those who were buried by its lava in the past, but the speaker announces that "It was pleasant to be sitting there" while the sultry "fulgurations" and the "flickering / Cast corners in the glass." He seems to have reduced the sublime possibilities to local and minor effects here, but he is quick to add that "He could describe / The terror of the sound," so we know that he is not hiding from the awesome power of a potential eruption. On the contrary, that threat seems to add to his pleasure. The speaker also recognizes that he appreciates the terror of the sound because "the sound / Was ancient." The volcano has a history to it, at least in human eyes, and its rumblings have gone on far longer than any individual human life.

The man's pleasure, then, is partially derived from his proximity to the potential terror of a volcanic eruption, just as the value of his lunch and the roses in the cool café are increased because of his awareness of pain and the knowledge that pain is totally human. The speaker's difference from the natural world is the point toward which the stanza moves, allowing the humanity of pain to be described in the following way:

> Except for us, Vesuvius might consume
> In solid fire the utmost earth and know
> No pain (ignoring the cocks that crow us up

To die). This is a part of the sublime
From which we shrink. And yet, except for us,
The total past felt nothing when destroyed.

Although it might seem that we should not be troubled by the fact that pain is human rather than natural, the speaker tells us otherwise, explaining that "This is a part of the sublime / From which we shrink." It is not simply that Vesuvius could "consume / In solid fire the utmost earth and know / No pain," even if that is slightly disconcerting; it is rather that the world, and Vesuvius, are *indifferent* to the pain we feel, whether it be the pain of everyday life or of a monstrous natural disaster. Pain is something *personal,* yet nature knows nothing of the individual.

Implicitly, Stevens is reminding us of the way in which the sublime has been denuded of its central context over the centuries: we have turned it into something purely glorious and ecstatic and stripped it of the terror and pain that are also an essential part of it. We have done this because we "shrink" from this part of the sublime, but there can be no sublime without the terror, and there can be no appreciation of the beautiful, or the "mal" of the world, without an understanding of the terror embodied in Vesuvius. Our sense of pain marks us as different, and thereby suggests our alienation from nature, but it also reminds us that there is to be no recompense for our pain: because it is ours rather than nature's, we shall not have our woes redressed by the world. Even worse, the pain that we experience in minor ways reveals the larger problem of being human. Stevens' sense of the sublime is based on the fact that "The volcano trembled in another ether, / As the body trembles at the end of life," so we know that the terror of the volcano has as much to do with our fear of death as it does with the daily pains of existence. We turn away from all of these things, even if we are aware at some level that our sense of values derives from our appreciation of these human facts.

Even if we were able to adjust to the terror of the sublime, however, we would find that our conceptions of human dignity were also called into question by it. We are affronted by the fact that the natural world is indifferent to us as individuals and cannot understand how this could be so. It goes against our sense of fair play, and we are so upset by the world's indifference that we have difficulty accepting it. The speaker's distress is registered via his perception of the moon, which

. . . rose up as if it had escaped
His meditation. It evaded his mind.

It was part of a supremacy always
Above him. The moon was always free from him,
As night was free from him. The shadow touched
Or merely seemed to touch him as he spoke
A kind of elegy he found in space. . . . (ii)

Because he desires his meditation to encompass everything, the speaker is not happy that the moon "rose up as if it had escaped / His meditation," though the "as if" suggests that whether it did indeed escape it remains in question. Regardless, it did evade his mind, and it was "part of a supremacy always / Above him." However powerful his mind might be, the moon—and the natural world of which it is a symbol—is always "above" him in the sense that its course and activity don't depend upon him in the least. Because the moon was "free from him," it was by definition beyond his control; because of this, the speaker feels alienated from the world. In his mind, only a world in which his own needs and wants were considered could be a happy one, so he is resentful that the world does evade him and is indifferent to him.

The cold indifference and supremacy of the moon return to face the other side of the problematic in that what really bothers the speaker is that the world cares nothing about his pain and suffering. Neither recompense nor understanding is offered, increasing the sense of alienation and blinding the man to the fact that the world's indifference is essential to his well being. As Stevens points out:

It is pain that is indifferent to the sky
In spite of the yellow of the acacias, the scent
Of them in the air still hanging heavily
In the hoary-hanging night. It does not regard
This freedom, this supremacy, and in
Its own hallucination never sees
How that which rejects it saves it in the end.

Humans tend to become absorbed in their own pain and suffering so much that they fail to recognize what the world would be like if the "moon" actually responded to their woes. Pain tends to focus everything upon the self, prompting one to ignore the "yellow of the acacias," leading one to forget "the scent / Of them in the air still hanging heavily / In the hoary-hanging night." Intensely focusing upon our own feelings, locked into our "own hallucination," we fail to note that "that which rejects [us] saves [us] in the end." Because the world is part of a supremacy always above us, it can draw us out of ourselves, pull us away from the powerful tug of our own feelings, lead us to consider something other than ourselves. In this way it saves us from the fate of being totally self-absorbed and reunites us with our world, albeit in a fashion that we find insufficient.

If the things of the world didn't exist in their own separate space, we would be incapable of appreciating their beauty, just as we wouldn't be able to discern what was and wasn't part of our space. The world's indifference allows us to discern the borders between our "selves" and the rest of the world, and this in turn allows us to appreciate properly those things the world has to offer us. Likewise, the shadow of the moon which "touched / Or merely seemed to touch" the speaker generates "A kind of elegy he found in space." The shadow of indifference reminds the speaker once again of his own death and the shadowy world of those no longer living, and it is this elegy that leads him to remember the value implicit in the world's indifference.

Stevens is not content merely to "construct a new stage," though; he also explains why humans have arrived at such a confused understanding of their world. If his own vision is straightforward enough—and it is—the only way to account for our inability regularly to perceive it is that the previous "stage" blinds us to the nature of what is, and for Stevens that earlier stage is Christianity. Now that "both heaven and hell / Are one, and here, O terra infidel" (iii), we don't know where we stand. We have destroyed the metaphysical world that created the older heaven and hell, but when we moved them onto our own planet, we didn't know how to integrate them into our vision. We might have dispensed with the solace of the religious vision, but what replaced that solace seemed to be nothing but pain and woe.

Of course, it is our *perception* of the world that makes it seem full of woe, and that perception is based upon the older model of things:

> The fault lies with an over-human god,
>
> Who by sympathy has made himself a man
>
> And is not to be distinguished, when we cry

> Because we suffer, our oldest parent, peer
> Of the populace of the heart, the reddest lord,
> Who has gone before us in experience.

We find that our model of god has all the flaws in it that the world itself never had. We want to create an "over-human world," but because we cannot do that—because the world always remains indifferent to us—we create an overhuman god instead, believing that such an invention will ease our pain because we will have a god who commiserates with us, in contrast to the world. In creating a god "Who by sympathy has made himself a man," we have left ourselves with a god who is "not to be distinguished" from humans. We think that is what we want, but gradually we come to learn that such a god diminishes rather than enhances our sense of value. Because he has always "gone before us in experience," we imagine he can relate to our woes, but in fact he only confirms the repetition of the woes of humanity and demonstrates their eternal return. In so doing, he doesn't help us to escape our pain; he only reinforces it by giving meaning to it. In the world itself, our pain has no meaning, which is as it should be; viewed through the "over-human god," our pain will always finally be recompensed, even if not here in this world.

The lack of distinction between the "reddest lord" and the human community thus demonstrates our desire for a world in which our pain makes sense, but if such a god makes sense of our pain and explains the evil of the world, he also reinforces our worst traits and contributes to a faulty picture of humanity. Stevens articulates this flaw when he says:

> If only he would not pity us so much,
> Weaken our fate, relieve us of woe both great
> And small, a constant fellow of destiny,
> A too, too human god, self-pity's kin
> And uncourageous genesis. . . .

The "uncourageous genesis" of this "too, too human god" is our own sense of self-pity. Because we pity ourselves, we imagine a god who can both understand our pain and redress it. Instead of relieving us of our woe, though, this god's pity merely reinforces our self-pity, making us worse rather than better, causing us to focus all the more vigorously on those things which seem to be wrong with the world we live in and prompting us to desire all the more fiercely a world in which those wrongs are righted.

Having "a constant fellow of destiny," one who confirms and justifies our pain, we think we have elaborated the ideal explanation for our existence. Our alienation from the world is overcome (seemingly), and the reasons for our discomfort are revealed. Likewise, we always have someone with whom we can commiserate about our fate and receive assurances that our grievances will be redressed. But this god doesn't make life easier but harder, and he doesn't strengthen us but rather "Weaken[s] our fate" precisely because he "relieve[s] us of woe both great / And small." In relieving us of our woe, he allows us to avoid dealing with the fact that no one can finally relieve us of it; he prompts us to think that there is an explanation for the pain of existence, which in turn leads us to think that everything has been comprehended and put into place. In Stevens' view, however, this god has weakened rather than strengthened our fate because he has allowed us to avoid what we are. We have not become stronger as human beings because we still haven't dealt with the inexplicability of our woes or the indifference of the world to them. We have thus avoided being fully human by failing to deal with those aspects of our existence we find most unappealing.

Of course, in the Christian view god is supposed to make us better humans precisely because he can empathize with our fate and can explain why we must suffer in this world. This vision is supposed to lead us to be better humans, to make good choices rather than bad ones, to help us understand that the pain will be dealt with at some later date. This makes our choices easier, for we have straightforward guidelines about what is good and bad, but it also diminishes the degree to which we actually participate in the values that make our lives, for so much has already been chosen for us. And in focusing our attention on the afterlife, when our woes will be redressed, this vision denies the value of *this* world, and hence is a negation of human values. Instead of helping us to choose to be wholly human, then, and instead of helping us accept the value and richness (and pain) of our condition, the too, too human god allows us to escape that which makes us human in the first place.

If our too human god does weaken our fate by allowing us to deny the facts of existence, the problem is that humans obviously have a difficult time accepting what they really are. They recoil from the prospect of having to accept themselves and their world and can make only tentative gestures in that direction, even when they realize the flaws of the over-human god. As Stevens put it:

It seems
As if the health of the world might be enough.
It seems as if the honey of common summer
Might be enough, as if the golden combs
Were part of a sustenance itself enough,
As if hell, so modified, had disappeared,
As if pain, no longer satanic mimicry,
Could be borne, as if we were sure to find our way.

It does indeed seem "As if the health of the world might be enough," but the "seems" clearly calls into question whether it *is* enough, just as the repetitions of "as if" undermine the other statements. Recognizing that we have created an over-human god, we should be satisfied with the world we have, we should find the honey of common summer to be enough, and we should be able to bear our pain once we discover that it is not a product of satanic mimicry but only an essential aspect of living. Equally, we should be able to "find our way" in this world without the guidance that we have previously thought necessary. But the very fact that we have created the over-human god suggests that perhaps all of these things are *not* enough; perhaps we are incapable of dealing with the world as it is rather than as we would like it to be. Certainly the gestures of the poem remain caught between the necessity of accepting the world as it is and the awareness that so far humans have been unable to do so.

"Esthétique du Mal" will continue to oscillate between the older, more nostalgic visions of the world and the new one that attempts to see it as it is, revealing in the process the ways in which we have tamed the world to make it seem a more liveable place, but the nostalgic visions grow more and more surreal and implausible. We have the sentimentalist in section IV who denudes nature of its horrifying aspects, the "Spaniard of the rose" who "rescue[s] the rose / From nature," but these gestures are futile. We can act as though the rose is not a part of the processes of life and death, just as we can continue to believe that somehow the evil of the world is not an intrinsic part of us—that it is somehow eradicable—but in the end we come back to its inevitable presence in the world. "The genius of misfortune / Is not a sentimentalist," as Stevens reminds us:

He is
That evil, that evil in the self, from which

In desperate hallow, rugged gesture, fault

Falls out on everything. . . . (iv)

Because evil is not outside of us but rather resides in the self, there is no denying it. Through the evil in the self "fault / Falls out on everything," and the only way to get rid of it would be to eliminate the self from which it comes. Instead of accepting this fact, though, we continue to allow the "genius of the body" to expend itself in "false engagements of the mind"; we move between locating the evil within us in the body or the mind at any given time, believing that if we could somehow determine its precise origin we could eliminate it. But this will never happen.

Stevens proposes instead to "let all true sympathizers come" to a different vision "Without the inventions of sorrow or the sob / Beyond invention" (v). Instead of beginning with the inventions of sorrow, which prompt us to imagine a world without pain, we must begin with what is and look for the compensations of life there:

Within what we permit,

Within the actual, the warm, the near,

So great a unity that it is bliss,

Ties us to those we love.

The poet consciously delimits the realm of the possible here, telling us that he wants to "permit" only certain things, but what he permits is what *is*—the only things that have been excluded are not in fact a part of the world anyway. Nevertheless, one must begin with the awareness of what one does not allow if one is to avoid imagining an unreal world. Within what is permitted, the most important aspects of life are part of "the warm, the near," in contrast to the cold and far of an otherworldly vision. Within the actual world in which we live the warm and the near provide the bliss of unity, that which ties us to other human beings and gives value to our everyday life. It is true that in many respects Stevens' work as a whole is strikingly devoid of other humans, and it has precious little to say about the value of love, but here he asserts the priority of love in human existence, implicitly claiming that it more than anything else ought to make the world enough for us.

The problem with the value of love, though, is that it depends upon gestures that are subtle and often difficult to distinguish, particularly when one has one's eyes focused on another world. It is, after all, the world of the familiar from which we try to escape, and so long as we try to remove ourselves from it we will miss the value of the smaller touches of love. For Stevens, the everyday world is more than sufficient, just as the love that provides its central value is more than enough:

> For this familiar
> This brother even in the father's eye,
> This brother half-spoken in the mother's throat
> And these regalia, these things disclosed,
> These nebulous brilliancies in the smallest look
> Of the being's deepest darling, we forego
> Lament, willingly forfeit the ai-ai
> Of parades in the obscurer selvages.

We have accustomed ourselves to a world in which we explore the "obscurer selvages" in the hope of finding a parade sufficiently grand to meet our expectations—we are always investigating the periphery for something that we think we might have missed. In so doing, we lose the value of that which is near, we miss the "thing disclosed" in the warmth of human relations, we dismiss the "nebulous brilliancies in the smallest look / Of the being's deepest darling." But the smallest look contains the greatest value within the near, even if it can only be discerned once we stop travelling to the obscurer selvages.

Human value is thus articulated out of the small acts of everyday life, the simple assertions that bring us in contact with other human beings, and Stevens shows the trade-off involved in focusing on these acts:

> Be near me, come closer, touch my hand, phrases
> Compounded of dear relation, spoken twice,
> Once by the lips, once by the services
> Of central sense, these minutiae mean more
> Than clouds, benevolences, distant heads.

"Be near me, come closer, touch my hand" are phrases that touch both the banality and the richness of everyday life. They are spoken often, yet they seldom are appreciated for what they imply. As part of the nearness of the actual, they are "Compounded of dear relation" in that they unite us both to others and within ourselves. The express both a physical relation and a mental one just as they mark out our relation to others. They are clearly only "minutiae," if one means by that that they are part of the typical aspects of everyday life, but for Stevens "these minutiae mean more / Than clouds, benevolences, distant heads" precisely because they are *here,* they are actual, instead of being distant or imaginary or non-existent. Value is articulated out of these minutiae, then, rather than out of the creation of clouds, benevolences, or distant heads that are escapes from value.

The minutiae of everyday life have always existed, and they have at least hypothetically always been enough, but we have chosen instead to project their value into another world, believing that if these phrases of dear relation somehow emanated from another, non-human source they would have more value. We created a fantastic, otherworldly display of potential glory and thereby diminished the value of the minutiae out of which it was developed. Stevens is merely reversing this process, bringing the value back to the minutiae out of which the glories of the otherworld were first established. For him human relation provides an "in-bar":

> Exquisite in poverty against the suns
>
> Of ex-bar, in-bar retaining attributes
>
> With which we vested, once, the golden forms
>
> And the damasked memory of the golden forms
>
> And ex-bar's flower and fire of the festivals
>
> Of the damasked memory of the golden forms,
>
> Before we were wholly human and knew ourselves.

The "golden forms" of religious ritual and ceremony have disappeared, even if the "damasked memory" of them hasn't, and now that they have come to nothing we are capable of seeing the way we vested them with attributes that were purely human. So while we might think that the disappearance of the golden forms of religion would also eliminate the positive attributes we projected into them, in fact the attributes return to us: we have lost nothing but the grand display in which these values were previously clothed and have gained a richer sense of the world at the same time. Now that we are "wholly human and [know] ourselves," we can see that the "flower and fire of the festivals" was simply our way of dressing up values that are more appropriate to the physical world in which our "wholly human" sensibility has come to locate itself at last. Of course Stevens assumes here that we have indeed finally become wholly human, an idea that is undercut by the question of whether this world will ever be enough for us or whether it only *seems* as though it *should* be enough, but the poem leaves no doubt that if we are truly to understand the aesthetic nature of our world and the evil that is inherent in it, we must begin by accepting a wholly human state rather than continuing to imagine that we are more than human and projecting our desires into a never-ending series of golden forms that deprives us of an appreciation of what we as humans do possess.

The chief difficulty in accepting our wholly human natures, of course, is that we must accede to our mortality; even more, to be wholly human we must come to see our mortality as part of the good of the world. We must, as Stevens does, take the red rose of the sentimentalist—a rose devoid of value and life precisely because it has been removed from the natural cycle of birth, growth, decay and death—and make it the rose of the "soldier's wound" (vii). "The soldier of time grown deathless in great size" believes that "his wound was good because life was." Pain may have been an inevitable part of his existence, but the pain was good because life itself was valuable. The soldier and his wound represent temporality, the wound of time that bleeds as our lives pass, confirming our mortality and defining for us the bounds of our possibilities. If we are to come to see the physical world as enough, we must perforce also come to accept the presence of the wound of time and find it too to be good.

. . . . . .

Even if we begin with the set of premises Stevens articulates in "Esthétique du Mal," though, we are still faced with the problem of how to reconfigure our world. We may have eliminated the golden forms of nostalgia, but we still need some kind of forms to make sense of our lives. The idea of evil demonstrates the difficulty, for even if we have killed off Satan and dissolved hell, that which Satan and hell represented still remains, and we have no way left to account for the space they occupied. It is not sufficient once they are gone to decide that there is no more evil, nor is it enough to project that evil onto other domains, as, for example, when we declare that "environmental influences" or "genetic factors" contribute to this or that person's "asocial" tendencies. These accounts of evil fail to deal with it adequately because they are so reductive and also because they are circular: if one decides that evil resides in environmental influences, then one will find it there.

Stevens poses this issue by stating quite properly that "The death of Satan was a tragedy / For the imagination" (viii). Satan occupied a rich imaginative space that symbolically accounted for the evil in the world, and even if we no longer believe in him, we must concede that the space he occupied has to be filled in some way, for if he is gone the phenomena for which he was to account remain behind. Even Satan's end reveals the necessity for some concept of evil:

> A capital
>
> Negation destroyed him in his tenement
>
> And, with him, many blue phenomena.
>
> It was not the end he had foreseen. He knew
>
> That his revenge created filial
>
> Revenges. And negation was eccentric.
>
> It had nothing of the Julian thunder-cloud:
>
> The assassin flash and rumble . . . He was denied.

As though it were a part of an urban renewal project, Satan's "tenement" was destroyed, and in the process "many blue phenomena" disappeared as well. We were no longer able to deal with those things he embodied. More strikingly, "It was not the end he had foreseen." Satan, after all, symbolizes more than anything else the human tendency for revenge and everything that is implied by that desire, and given this, he could have expected at the very least to be killed by a masterful act of revenge. Just as he tried to usurp the "Julian" throne of god, overturning it via his own act of revenge, so he might imagine that he too would be overturned either by god or else by someone else who wanted to assert the same kind of priority. But his death had nothing of the "Julian thunder-cloud" about it; there wasn't even any "assassin flash and rumble." Instead, he was simply denied. No great battle, no confirmation of the vengeful tendencies he symbolized. He was quietly written out of existence.

As Stevens points out here, Satan, as the embodiment of revenge, knows that "his revenge created filial revenges": the drive for priority and power continues among us all the time. Likewise, Satan knows that "negation [is] eccentric": there is no telling exactly upon whom the vengeful tendencies will be visited, for they are often displaced onto another rather than being directed at the object of vengeance. Even so, in some fashion Satan's death should have displayed the full power of vengeance and its hidden desires, yet he seemed to disappear without any excitement at all, leaving, seemingly, no trace behind.

The denial of Satan might have been a quiet move, without the "assassin flash and rumble," but the desire for revenge and the consequences of that desire have not disappeared. We are simply left unable to account for them. In this we are worse rather than better off, and this is why the death of Satan *was* a tragedy for the imagination. Stevens puts the matter this way:

> Phantoms, what have you left? What underground?
>
> What place in which to be is not enough
>
> To be? You go, poor phantoms, without place
>
> Like silver in the sheathing of the sight,
>
> As the eye closes. . . .

If Satan is the symbolic embodiment of our desire for revenge, that desire has its origin in the negation that declares that "to be is not enough / To be." Humans have never been satisfied simply with being; that has not been enough. They have always wanted *more,* and that "more" is usually established in terms of kinds of priority: this or that has *more* than I do, so I want to usurp its place. Satan was not content to be, even though he was one of the highest members of the celestial hierarchy; he wanted more, wanted to be at the top of the hierarchy and thus committed his act of revenge in the hope of overcoming the priority of god. This negation of the one who is seen to have priority over us is indeed "eccentric" because it can project itself readily onto other objects, but it is the negation that drives the human dissatisfaction with existence, and it remains behind once Satan is gone.

The "phantoms" seem to have left nothing behind. There is no longer an "underground" that marks out the space for human dissatisfaction, and Satan himself has disappeared. Thus, there seems to be no place left in which "to be is not enough / To be." But the phantom of revenge, the desire for more and the negation that drives that desire, hasn't disappeared; it has simply become homeless. The "poor phantoms" wander "without place / Like silver in the sheathing of the sight." We cannot locate them, and they almost seem to be hallucinatory as a result, but they still exist. We have displaced them, but that has only kept us from being able to explain our desire for negation, our will-to-death. It might have been heroic to deny Satan, but this act only confirmed his continuing presence. The irony, of course, is that one would think the denial of heaven would have the most profound impact upon humans, yet the denial of hell is more important because it leaves us unable to account for the desire that created heaven in the first place.

Humans face a double loss in the negation of the golden forms, then. Their desire for another world is shattered, and they are left with no way to account for the evil of the world. And without a way to account for the "mal" of the world, desire as negation will continue to float homelessly either until it is understood or until yet another series of golden forms is established. Before we realize the loss of Satan, after all, we recognize the loss of our hopes for a perfect world:

> How cold the vacancy
>
> When the phantoms are gone and the shaken realist
>
> First sees reality. The mortal no
>
> Has its emptiness and tragic expirations.

When the phantoms disappear, the "shaken realist" can't help but feel the cold vacancy of the world and notice its emptiness. Heaven and hell were the twin embodiments of his desire for something more—heaven as that state of pure death in which desire no longer yearns for more, hell as that state in which negation can delude one into imagining one's own priority in the world. Without these two states, the world seems barren indeed, cold and devoid of value. But the real problem is not the "mortal no" itself, though that is often what we are told; it is that

> The tragedy . . . may have begun,
>
> Again, in the imagination's new beginning,
>
> In the yes of the realist spoken because he must
>
> Say yes, spoken because under every no
>
> Lay a passion for yes that had never been broken.

The realist is usually attacked because his "mortal no" seems to be a cynical negation of everything of value in the world and a denial of all those things humans have deemed most important. But the real potential for tragedy is hidden in the fact that the realist's "no" is based upon "a passion for yes that had never been broken." The "yes" underlying the "no" of the realist is the desire to affirm life, in itself the central assertion of human value. But if the realist cannot create forms to make sense of the underground of Satan, his passion for yes might well simply end up engendering yet another set of religious forms that once again denies the value of the world.

The essential struggle for the realist, then, has nothing at all to do with his desire to negate the false structures of an earlier epoch—that is his strength. The struggle has to do with how he reacts to the world that is left behind after the negations, and how he puts his affirmation of life into play in the world. The realist's first reaction is "Panic in the face of the moon,"

> . . . panic, because
>
> The moon is no longer these nor anything
>
> And nothing is left but comic ugliness
>
> Or a lustred nothingness. (ix)

Once the moon is stripped of its symbolic clothing, it seems to be nothing at all, either a "comic ugliness" or a "lustred nothingness." The panic that is generated by this sense of vacancy and void might well prompt the realist to return to that which he has already negated, for the desire for more has not disappeared—only the symbolic embodiment of it has. The realist still needs, desires, more, but now he seems to have no way of achieving it. The physical world doesn't seem to be enough for him, and he immediately loses sight of the value this world has.

If the realist can overcome his panic, though, he can see the double compensations that are offered to him by the natural world. First of all, "he / That has lost the folly of the moon becomes / The prince of the proverbs of pure poverty." Without imposing artificial meanings upon the natural objects of the world and turning them into metaphysical manifestations, one has stripped the "moon" of all of its Romantic and nostalgic associations and is left with the "proverbs of pure poverty." These proverbs speak of what is in the natural world without turning it into something it isn't, and if that means one has an impoverished vision of the world, it is at least a purer view of things. Even more, such a vision focuses on the miraculous nature of the mundane:

> To lose sensibility, to see what one sees,

As if sight had not its own miraculous thrift,
To hear only what one hears, one meaning alone,
As if the paradise of meaning ceased
To be paradise, it is this to be destitute.

Our senses are extraordinary in their own right, having, among other things, their "own miraculous thrift." They sense precisely and focus clearly without any prompting from us, and if this world of the senses strips the "paradise of meaning" to only one level and leaves us "destitute," still it manifests a paradise in its own way. By employing the "as if" here again, Stevens reminds us that of course the paradise of meaning doesn't cease—even the sounds we hear that are stripped of the golden forms still carry meaning, for that is what differentiates them from mere noise. And the miraculous thrift of sight and sound is a condensation of meaning all its own. Nevertheless, this stripped version of the world at least divests the sky "of its fountains" and accepts that the "indifferent crickets chant / Through our indifferent crises." They offer no prophetic utterances and promise nothing to alleviate our crises or eliminate our pain, and this is why the vision of the physical world is "destitute."

The world of ordinary sense perception, however, may be one part of the world when it is reduced to a near approximation of what is, but this alone is not enough for humans. They may be dazzled to some degree by the miraculous nature of their senses, even as they may appreciate the beauty inherent in nature. But this is not enough to satisfy the desire for more:

Yet we require
Another chant, an incantation, as in
Another and later genesis, music
That buffets the shapes of its possible halcyon
Against the haggardie . . . A loud, large water
Bubbles up in the night and drowns the crickets' sound.
It is a declaration, a primitive ecstasy,
Truth's favors sonorously exhibited.

If our senses tie us to the world, they still require a deeper level of connection, some kind of "primitive ecstasy" in which "Truth's favors

[are] sonorously exhibited." The physical world also provides this, here in the "loud, large water [that] / Bubbles up in the night and drowns the crickets' sound." The bubbling of the water from deep within the earth provides "Another chant, an incantation" that offers us the same ecstatic vision that the golden forms provide through religious ritual and rite. The crickets' sound is the everyday perception of the world, and it predominates, but the bubbling water also appears and affords us the primitive and communal vision of the world that we find necessary to satisfy our desire for more than the everyday. Neither the sound of the crickets nor the bubbling of water is a compensation for the religious forms we have left behind—they are the sounds out of which the religious forms were generated in the first place, and once we return to them we can see how they offer us almost everything the golden forms did. They lack only the sense of metaphysical meaning that we also think we need.

. . . . . .

The golden forms of religion, however, are not only embodied in Christianity; they also appear in other guises, many of which anthropomorphize the natural world itself. Thus, the poet must investigate the artificial ways we have imposed meaning on nature, and Stevens chooses to play with the cliché of Mother Earth to explore these meanings. As with all clichés, there is some value inherent in "Mother Earth," and the poet seeks to extract it while leaving its absurdities behind:

> He had studied the nostalgias.
>
> He sought the most grossly maternal, the creature
>
> Who most fecundly assuaged him, the softest
>
> Woman with a vague moustache and not the mauve
>
> *Maman.* His anima liked its animal
>
> And liked it unsubjugated, so that home
>
> Was a return to birth, a being born
>
> Again in the savagest severity,
>
> Desiring fiercely, the child of a mother fierce
>
> In his body, fiercer in his mind, merciless
>
> To accomplish the truth in his intelligence. (x)

Instead of imagining a mother figure that would embody only what we traditionally have thought of as feminine traits, the poet wants his Mother Earth to have a "vague moustache"—she must have her share of testosterone too and not simply be composed of the female hormones. Instead of the nostalgic image of a docile, succoring mother, the poet wants his "anima" to be "unsubjugated," both by myth and by meaning. She should not be stripped of the other aspects of the natural world, for if she is to represent the processes of birth as well as earthly life, she must evoke the "savagest severity" of the processes of life, must embrace a process in which "Desiring fiercely" is as much a function of life as is comfort. This "grossly maternal" figure thus "fecundly assuage[s] him" not by hiding the savage severity of birth and life but by fully revealing it; she comforts him by disclosing his unsubjugated anima and by demonstrating that he is "the child of a mother fierce / In his body, fiercer in his mind." The fierce, unsubjugated process of life exists in both his body and his mind; he doesn't restrict its force to his animal activities or his physical existence. The same severity that dominates the bodily processes also imbues his mind, which is "merciless / To accomplish the truth in his intelligence." His desire to know what is rather than to be content with illusion emanates from the savage severity of his unsubjugated anima as much as any bodily desire does.

The grossly maternal vision the poet advocates contrasts with the "other mothers" we have invented over the millennia, but Stevens argues that the "she-wolves / And forest tigresses and women mixed with the sea" "were fantastic," unbelievable exaggerations both of the natural world and of human disposition. They may have embodied part of the physical world, but in taking that part to excess they fantasized a world that was either better or worse than the one in which we actually live. Even more, they offered meanings and explanations that were false to life. Stevens' "softest woman," then, is not soft in the traditional sense at all; she is fierce and unsubjugated. She is soft only because "she is as she was, reality, / The gross, the fecund," and that is enough. Precisely because she is reality, because she is both gross and fecund, she "proved him against the touch / Of impersonal pain." The poet doesn't ask for the illusions of the past; his softest woman explains without being reduced to a goddess or a nymph.

The older, nostalgic vision of nature was based on an explanation of life that made sense out of the pain and evil in the world and compensated for it by being so softly maternal and caring. Stevens' vision of the "softest woman" also "prove[s] him against the touch / Of impersonal pain," but it achieves this in a different way. If "Reality explained," it does so by revealing "the last nostalgia: that he / Should understand." Human pain still exists, and it is still "impersonal" in the sense that nature has nothing to do with it at all, but in Stevens' world there are no justifications for or explanations of it. On the contrary, for the poet the grossly maternal figure proves him against the touch of impersonal pain by revealing to him that there is no reason for it. She disabuses him of the final nostalgia, that he should be able to understand why there is pain and why it comes in the forms it does. There *is* no explanation, and the poet is comforted by this rather than distressed:

> That he might suffer or that
>
> He might die was the innocence of living, if life
>
> Itself was innocent. To say that it was
>
> Disentangled him from sleek ensolacings.

"Mother Earth" explains that human suffering and death are simply part of the "innocence of living"; they do not *mean* anything, nor do they fit into a larger plan of recompense and reversal. They simply *are;* they are part of being human, no more, no less.

At the same time, Stevens again makes clear that this consoling vision itself might be based on illusion. Suffering and death *may* be part of the innocence of living, but this presupposes that life itself is innocent. There is no way for us to know whether it is or not, and the poet concedes that. Thus, the grossly maternal vision might rest upon an illusion, but for the poet it is enough that this possible illusion "Disentangles him from sleek ensolacings." Even if it is false, the idea that life is innocent keeps him from being seduced by even greater illusions: that suffering and death have meaning and purpose, that there is a reason for everything that he does and that is done to him. Humans can never assume that they know reality as it is; they can only do the best they can to understand the world as it is. In studying the nostalgias, after all, Stevens works out of a vision of Mother Earth, and if he strips this construct of the illusions he perceives in it, he also recognizes that it remains a construct in the end. To see the earth as a grossly maternal creature is to give some meaning to it, when the world itself is outside of the domain of human meaning. The poet has never left the world of meaning itself; he has only tried to revise the meanings, and as such he concedes from the beginning that he cannot escape from the potential illusions of language.

We must also keep in mind, though, that Stevens is not suggesting here that language is *necessarily* false. It always carries with it that potential, and we can never know for certain whether or not what it tells us is truth or illusion, but it displays the capacity for truth as well as illusion. In the next section of the poem Stevens proclaims "Natives of poverty, children of malheur, / The gaiety of language is our seigneur" (xi), and this statement bears the complex sense of language and its relation to the world that the poet wants to articulate. Stevens doesn't say that *language* is our "seigneur"; he insists that the *gaiety* of language is our seigneur, and it is that gaiety that is the mark of the truth value of language, that which confirms its approximation to reality. Language remains a human construct, but we are guided by the gaiety—by the aesthetic appropriateness—of its statements, and through this aesthetic our "malheur" and "poverty" are both revealed and enriched. In contrast to instrumental uses of language that are stripped of the aesthetic and dominated by our will, the aesthetic uses of language place us in the subordinate position: the aesthetic masters us rather than the other way around, and any truths that are available to us come from this manifestation of words. Language forces us to conclude that "Life is a bitter aspic," that "We are not / At the centre of a diamond," but the aesthetic vision of the world that is articulated through the gaiety of language allows us to make the most of our position on the planet.

Having established the "impoverished" vision of the world upon which his aesthetic is based, Stevens must also deal with the interests of the self as they intersect this world. The traditional dilemma about the relation between self and other has yet to be overcome, so he returns to it to reveal its fatuity:

> He disposes the world in categories, thus:
> The peopled and the unpeopled. In both, he is
> Alone. But in the peopled world, there is,
> Besides the people, his knowledge of them. In
> The unpeopled, there is his knowledge of himself.
> Which is more desperate in the moments when
> The will demands that what he thinks be true? (xii)

The speaker of the poem begins by perceiving himself as essentially isolated. The two categories of peopled and unpeopled trap him into a perspective in which he is alone regardless of which world he chooses. In the one he has knowledge of others, in the other knowledge of himself, but finally both of them are "desperate" worlds when it comes to the "will [that] demands that what he thinks be true." Because the world has been made binary from the beginning, the sense of either of these views is bound to be false precisely because it excludes the other. Either way, the speaker is thus both isolated *and* desperate: he cannot escape from his total alienation, and he must conclude that any knowledge he might have will inevitably be illusory.

The only way around the dilemma of self and other is to see it in all its absurdity, and the speaker proceeds to do just that when he attempts to locate the kind of knowledge available to each part of the world:

> Is it himself in them that he knows or they
>
> In him? If it is himself in them, they have
>
> No secret from him. If it is they in him,
>
> He has no secret from them. This knowledge
>
> Of them and of himself destroys both worlds,
>
> Except when he escapes from it. To be
>
> Alone is not to know them or himself.

The questioning here demonstrates that neither possibility works. The speaker doesn't know himself in "them," nor do they know him in them. Just as clearly, he has secrets from others and they have secrets from him, so he inevitably concludes that "The knowledge / Of them and of himself destroys both worlds," leaving him again outside of a world in which he understands. "Except," he says, "when he escapes from it." The knowledge he possesses cancels itself out, and he escapes from its clutches, recognizing that "To be / Alone is not to know them or himself." If he is indeed a totally alienated being, he knows nothing about nothing, for such a creature by definition is locked into a solipsistic vision in which knowledge is impossible. He must thus conclude both that simple being itself provides no knowledge and that it is impossible to be "alone" in the isolated sense he imagined.

Emptying out both the world of self and the world of the other, the speaker realizes, "creates a third world without knowledge, / In which no one peers, in which the will makes no / Demands." This third world that is devoid of knowledge is arrived at only after one has abandoned the binarism upon which the earlier dilemma was based, and it offers one the aesthetic perception that allows one to see the world as it is without the incessant demands of the will for human meaning. In this third world, the will

> . . . accepts whatever is as true,
>
> Including pain, which, otherwise, is false.
>
> In the third world, then, there is no pain.

In accepting whatever is as true, the will also manages to escape pain, at least as it is traditionally defined, for it makes no attempt to attribute meaning to or justification for the pain. It simply is, and any other explanation of what pain is "is false." It exists, is part of what is, and nothing more can be said about it.

It would seem that once again the problem of pain and the difficulty of knowledge have been dealt with thoroughly, but this account of the way things are ignores human relationships. Even if this third world establishes a domain without knowledge and pain, it hardly eliminated the basic problems of life. As Stevens says: "Yes, but / What lover has one in such rocks, what woman, / However known, at the centre of the heart?" The human world of friends and lovers is different than the purely physical world, and no one is capable of establishing relationships solely on the basis of the vision of the third world—it is a vision that connects us to the physical world, but it remains incapable of dealing with the difficulties of human intercourse. It seems as though there is no one vision of the world that can account at the same time for the phenomena of the physical and the human world, for social being is by definition full of meaning. The best that can be hoped for is a different understanding of the social world that is based on the vision of the third world without pain and knowledge, the kind of understanding that Stevens pursues in the next section of the poem when he considers the individual human life.

. . . . . .

In the physical world, there is no pain, if it be properly perceived, but in the social world there *is* evil, the cultural equivalent of pain. And no aesthetics of "mal" can be sufficient if it fails to encompass the evil of the social world as well. Stevens' approach to this domain is, as it was with Mother Nature, through a traditional explanation of the evil in the social world, but he quickly dispenses with this account:

It may be that one life is a punishment
For another, as the son's life for the father's.
But that concerns the secondary characters.
It is a fragmentary tragedy
Within the universal whole. (xiii)

There are two ways of arguing that "one life is a punishment / For another." First, the view that reciprocation and fair play are part of the universe would suggest to some that what goes unpunished in one life will be paid for in another. More importantly, as the "son's life for the father's" suggests, we can see how the reciprocal revenge in which people involve themselves—most obviously between father and son—can cause the son's life to be a punishment for the father's. In imitating the father's vengeful tendencies as they were inflicted upon him, the son returns the father's violence to him, but in the process he doesn't escape from the revenge his father inflicted upon him—he only exacerbates it and participates in it more fully than his father. Thus, his own life ends up being a punishment for what the father did to him, as in the basic Oedipal context.

Stevens acknowledges that such vicious circles might work themselves out within the human community, but even that acknowledgment is hedged by the "It may be." And regardless, he dismisses such reciprocation by stating that "that concerns the secondary characters": even if such things do happen, they are only part of "a fragmentary tragedy / Within the universal whole." In other words, the localized exchange of vengeance is less important in the larger context of the world as a whole than the fact that

The son
And the father alike and equally are spent,
Each one, by the necessity of being
Himself, the unalterable necessity
Of being this unalterable animal.

Humans may well perpetually act out of a reciprocal desire for revenge, and this is indeed the course of human evil, but the source of that desire lies even deeper, in the necessity each one of us has of "being / Himself." The difficulty inherent in the necessity of being oneself is that it *is* a necessity, and it is based upon "the unalterable necessity / Of being this unalterable animal." We cannot escape from our animal natures, even if we can think and imagine; even more, we cannot escape from the unalterability of our natures. We may well be able to change some things about our lives, but any such changes must be based upon the unalterable necessity of being basically both unalterable and animal. We are capable of changing much less about ourselves than we think, and only when we begin to face the true aspects of our nature can we see how much this is so.

Our inability to change either the necessity of being ourselves or the essentially unalterable animal nature we possess is the origin of the most difficult human problems. As Stevens says: "This force of nature in action is the major / Tragedy. This is destiny unperplexed, / The happiest enemy." The force of nature of which he speaks is the combined problematic of needing to be oneself and being essentially unalterable at the same time. The two aspects of our being conflict because our knowledge of the necessity of being ourselves prompts us to want to be something other, yet the more we try to be other than what we are, the more we are faced with our unalterability. This is the "major tragedy" both because it makes us perpetually unhappy with what we are and because our desire to be something other than what we are perpetuates the vengefulness, the desire to negate and deny that is the source of human evil. This is the domain that Satan left uninhabited when he disappeared; this is "destiny unperplexed" because it accounts for the way we behave and explains why we are spent by the necessity of being ourselves. It takes all we have simply to work through this bind, and yet we seldom manage to escape it. This is "the happiest enemy" only because he can indeed be found and does indeed account for our behavior. He remains tragic chiefly because we spend ourselves trying to defeat him and can never do so. We are unwilling to see our actions in such "unperplexed" terms, though these are the necessities that drive us even if we remain unaware of them.

The human desire to be something else and the necessity to be "this unalterable animal" are aspects of existence that must be accounted for in any aesthetic, at least as far as Stevens is concerned, because his is a worldly rather than an otherworldly aesthetic, and it must thus articulate the beautiful in its relation to both the good and the evil in human life. This aesthetic contrasts with precisely what Stevens has pointed out here, for the traditional vision of beauty is one that allows us to escape the knowledge of our necessities momentarily, allows us to forget about the unalterability of our animal natures. The Romantic aesthetic becomes part of the problem in that its vision of purity and beauty prompts us to loathe our selves all the more, thereby inducing us to try all the harder to be something other than we are. Stevens' aesthetic is based upon the necessity of accepting what we are, for seeing the beautiful in the necessities that govern our lives as well as in the freedom from those necessities. The world of the beautiful and the good is not separate from the world of pain and evil; it is part of the same space and must be seen in that context. Thus,

> . . . it may be
>
> That in his Mediterranean cloister a man,
>
> Reclining, eased of desire, establishes
>
> The visible, a zone of blue and orange
>
> Versicolorings, establishes a time
>
> To watch the fire-feinting sea and calls it good,
>
> The ultimate good, sure of a reality
>
> Of the longest meditation, the maximum,
>
> The assassin's scene.

The man who is capable of reclining "eased of desire" might well be able to establish the visible, declare it real and see it as the ultimate good, but that is the *easy* part. It is not enough to see the world as it is and to accept it as the ultimate good simply because it is; one must also see that at the heart of this "maximum" vision of the world lies "The assassin's scene." If we are to accept the world as it is and declare it the ultimate good because it is what we have, we must also see that

> Evil in evil is
>
> Comparative. The assassin discloses himself,
>
> The force that destroys us is disclosed, within
>
> This maximum, an adventure to be endured
>
> With the politest helplessness. Ay-mi!
>
> One feels its action moving in the blood.

We have wanted to see the world of the beautiful and the good as a world of freedom from ourselves and our evil, but if we are to establish the "maximum" aesthetic Stevens creates, we must see that "The force that destroys us is disclosed, within / This maximum." That which undercuts our lives is not something that is visited upon us from the outside, nor is it something that can be avoided. It is a part of the ultimate good, even if that which destroys us means that evil and finitude and mortality will not go away.

At least as troubling to us is the fact that this world of the ultimate good is based upon "an adventure to be endured / With the politest helplessness." Far from being a place where we can escape from necessity, the world is such that our adventure is based in large part simply on enduring the life that we have and accepting its necessities with "the politest helplessness." Rather than fighting against that about which we can do nothing, we must learn to accept the unalterability of our selves, and until we can do that we shall remain incapable of seeing the world as the ultimate good. Even if we resist this knowledge, however, we can still feel "its action moving in the blood." We can sense within ourselves and our bodily functions the assassin that is part of the scene, and we cannot avoid sensing this simply because we are bodily creatures. The only choice we have is to accept or to ignore what the action moving in our blood tells us.

Our resistance to the knowledge we possess within ourselves is so strong, though, that we have been almost successful in ignoring it for millennia, if always only *almost* successful. In the end, of course, we must accept what we know to be true simply because we all must finally die. Our modes of resistance against the knowledge we already possess occur in various domains both local and general. The fight between father and son—the revenge upon which so much of our lives is based—is certainly the primary social means through which we seek to escape our knowledge and obtain priority at the same time. But this force is not restricted to local fields or particular problems: it also appears in the larger domains as well in our desire for a metaphysic that will allow us to transcend the necessities of our lives and in the political visions we generate out of such metaphysics. This is the last human domain with which Stevens must deal if his aesthetic of "mal" is to be complete, and he turns to it in section XIV, exploring the implications of these desires in terms of yet another metaphor, what we might call "the Idea of Geneva," at least as Geneva was imagined in the earlier part of the twentieth century, when it became the locus of various philosophers and politicians.

The initial context upon which the section is based is the Russian Revolution and all that it connotes, though Stevens brings Russia into play indirectly by quoting from an external source:

> Victor Serge said, "I followed his argument
> With the blank uneasiness which one might feel
> In the presence of a logical lunatic."
> He said it of Konstantinov. Revolution
> Is the affair of logical lunatics.

Victor Serge obviously felt that the fervor with which Konstantinov was able to deny the existence of reality reflected what he calls a "logical lunatic." The ideas through which he sees the world are so intense that their logic blocks out everything that doesn't correspond to them. So too, Stevens argues, "Revolution / Is the affair of logical lunatics." In order to contemplate the complete transformation of society, one has to be so overwhelmed by the force of one's ideas that one forgets what human nature and society are truly like. In the present context, it is not just the fervor with which one wishes one's ideas were possible that blinds the individual; it is also the naiveté about what can and cannot be changed in the human situation. A logical lunatic who imagines that society can be totally transformed to reflect an egalitarian state where there is no government, for example, has lost sight of the unalterable aspects of humans, has forgotten their animal nature and their past—which is never so easily eradicable as logical lunatics like to imagine—and has also ignored the fact that most of human behavior is driven by the desire which says that "to be is not enough to be." If humans are driven by that desire, then *no* state is going to satisfy them, even if it were possible to create one that was truly egalitarian. Thus, even if the logic of the political creed is irrefragable, the application of it results in lunacy simply because it takes no account of what actually is.

Most revolutionaries, though, are aware at least in part of the lunacy of their ideas and do their best to keep this knowledge from others: "The politics of emotion must appear / To be an intellectual structure." In general the lunacy of the ideas derives from the fact that the concepts are based on the "politics of emotion" rather than on an analysis of what is and what is possible; in order to hide the emotion that generates the ideas in the first place, revolutionaries in this view create a politics that *appears* to be "an intellectual structure." "The cause / Creates a logic not to be distinguished / From lunacy" both because it is originally based on emotion rather than logic and because its logic bears little relation to the world in which it is to be applied. Stevens is not arguing against the possibility of societal change here, but he is suggesting that any possible changes must develop out of what is and what is possible rather than out a fervent desire to fill up permanently the hole of desire. The unreality of "revolutionary" ideas dooms them to failure, or worse, to the implementation of greater evil than that which they were supposedly designed to overcome.

While Konstantinov is the primary example used in this section of the poem, philosopher logicians are also being attacked here. After all, Geneva was the site of great philosophical speculation at the beginning of the century, and most of it had to do with either logic or the uses of language. Hence, Stevens adds:

> One wants to be able to walk
>
> By the lake at Geneva and consider logic:
>
> To think of the logicians in their graves
>
> And of the worlds of logic in their great tombs.
>
> Lakes are more reasonable than oceans.

If one were to walk by the lake at Geneva and consider logic and the logicians of the twentieth century, one would, among other things, find not only the "logicians in their graves" but also the "worlds of logic in their great tombs." Their tombs contain their logic as well as their mortal remains, for, like Konstantinov, their logic was finally based upon a lunacy, chiefly the notion that the world could be reduced to logic, and then built up and explained from that base. If the logicians were aware of their surroundings, they would have noticed that they were capable of imagining their logical schemes because they contemplated them in the context of a lake, and lakes are always "more reasonable than oceans" because they are contained and conceptualizable. One can walk around their borders and see to the other side, and the illusion of containment that a reasonable lake would offer might prompt logicians to imagine that the human world was rather lake-like too, that there was nothing of the ocean in human nature. Of course, the unfathomability of the ocean is a more appropriate symbol for the unfathomability of human beings, but then the logicians would never notice that because they didn't want to accept the complexity of the world.

The problem of the logicians and the revolutionaries, though, goes deeper than that, and again, a walk around the lake at Geneva would reveal this in a moment. Stevens points out that

A promenade amid the grandeurs of the mind,
By a lake, with clouds like lights among great tombs,
Gives one a blank uneasiness, as if
One might meet Konstantinov, who would interrupt
With his lunacy.

The "grandeurs of the mind"—even considered on a promenade by a lake—give "one a blank uneasiness" simply because most of the grand ideas have as studiously ignored the world as has any revolutionary ideology. Most were generated out of a desire to deny what is rather than to articulate the nature of the world; most set out to overcome the limits of human nature and fulfill the unfulfillable creature; most attempted to free humans from enslavement rather than to establish the ways in which we are bound and unalterable. The "grandeurs of the mind" are based on their own lunacy, a madness not to be distinguished from the more obvious ideologies.

The figure of Konstantinov embraces more than political revolutionaries, then, just as he embodies more than logicians and those devoted to the "grandeurs of the mind"; finally he represents all those humans who live their lives through the lunacy of illusory ideas. If Konstantinov were walking by the lake,

He would not be aware of the lake.
He would be the lunatic of one idea
In a world of ideas, who would have all the people
Live, work, suffer and die in that idea
In a world of ideas. He would not be aware of the clouds,
Lighting the martyrs of logic with white fire.
His extreme of logic would be illogical.

Humans are so preoccupied with their desire—so taken up with the notion that "to be is not enough to be"—that they tend in their own ways to become "lunatic[s] of one idea," and in turn they imagine a world where *everyone* "Live[s], work[s], suffer[s] and die[s] in that idea / In a world of ideas." They are so repulsed by the world in which they live—and by the possibility of being truly human—that they would prefer to deny everything they don't approve of and imagine another world with richer possibilities. In so doing, they both deny their own natures and lose sight of "the clouds": the external world disappears along with the internal one, and they are left locked within the confines of an illogical lunacy that captivates them throughout their life. In being unable to bear their own humanity and the "rejection" of the external world, they fail to see how they create their own alienation through the world they imagine just as they ignore the fact that "that which rejects [them] (the physical world) saves [them] in the end."

Having established the parameters of human existence as he sees them, Stevens has also demarcated both an aesthetic and an ethic, and thus in contrast to his forebears he has an aesthetic that accounts for the beautiful and the good *and* the evil as well. This aesthetic is finally based on a very simple premise, one that Stevens saves for the end precisely because it is so simple:

> The greatest poverty is not to live
>
> In a physical world, to feel that one's desire
>
> Is too difficult to tell from despair. (xv)

In contrast to his earlier uses of poverty—where the impoverished vision was the "realist's" because he stripped the world of its golden forms and pleasant illusions—now Stevens asserts that the greatest poverty is "not to live / In a physical world." The entire poem has been directed toward this reversal, as we have seen again and again how those who perceive the world through golden forms—or through the logical lunacy of one idea—have both created a false sense of things and denied the value of life at the same time. This is truly the greatest poverty, for choosing to imagine what isn't and will never be prevents one from appreciating that which is. Of course in Stevens' view one can no longer deny those aspects of existence or human nature that one would prefer to ignore, but existence and human nature are better valued because those things we have chosen to deny are seen in the context of a much larger vision, one that subsumes that "evil" into the broader domain in the aesthetic itself. At the end of the poem Stevens leaves no doubt that the trade-offs involved in this change of vision clearly favor the person who chooses to be "wholly human" and live in the physical world.

Equally important, Stevens has located the fatal flaw of the world of illusions: it leads one finally "to feel that one's desire / Is too difficult to tell from despair." The lunatics of one idea and the proponents of the golden forms would have us believe that their visions offer us the fulfillment of our desires, and hence allow us to escape from our despair. In fact, though, their visions of fulfilled desire are really only displaced images of death, hence in the end "too difficult to tell from despair." They are simply the images of our despair written into more pleasing forms. Nevertheless, if it is time, mortality and human evil that make us despair, all of the golden forms only re-present us with that same temporality, mortality and evil—they simply disguise it.

The world of golden forms denies this world, projects our desires for stasis and immortality into a world stripped of all its physical attributes. As such, it denies what we are and what we have. And even if these forms didn't deny the life we have, what they have to offer as a replacement is less than sufficient. As Stevens points out:

> Perhaps,
>
> After death, the non-physical people, in paradise,
>
> Itself non-physical, may, by chance, observe
>
> The green corn gleaming and experience
>
> The minor of what we feel.

There are no more guarantees for the world after death than there are for the world of the living, but even if there were, the best that could be said is that *perhaps* such non-physical people in a non-physical world would be able to "observe / The green corn gleaming," and even then they would only experience "The minor of what we feel" because they would not be connected to the processes of life and death and sensory perception that allow the proper appreciation of something as commonplace yet pleasing as the gleaming of the green corn. Stripped of a sense of time and decay, cut off from that which makes value possible in the first place, such non-physical people could hardly experience the intensity of the corn the way an ordinary mortal can.

Instead of these dim and finally unsatisfactory future possibilities, Stevens wants to redirect our attention, for there is one way of looking at the world that humans have never seriously tried before, the one Stevens urges upon us: "The adventurer / In humanity has not conceived of a race / Completely physical in a physical world." The civilizations of the world—and particularly the West—have been quite "adventurous" and have imagined all sorts of explanations of the world and what it holds for us, but in spite of all our adventurousness, we have yet to explore the one vision that has been available to humanity from the start; we have not yet been willing to imagine "a race / Completely physical in a physical world," and that is what Stevens proposes we must do if we are ever to come to grips with our own natures and with the world as it truly is.

A race that was completely physical in a physical world would confront a new terrain:

> The green corn gleams and the metaphysicals
>
> Lie sprawling in majors of the August heat,
>
> The rotund emotions, paradise unknown.

The green corn would still gleam for such a people, but that would not be all they would see. The "metaphysicals [would] / Lie sprawling in majors of the August heat" as well. The metaphysical world would not simply be denied any more than it would be embraced; it would be written into the physical world, from which it originally came. Stripped of the human desire to escape this world, and returned to its own proper location, the corn and the metaphysicals would generate "The rotund emotions, paradise unknown." Instead of reducing our emotions and our sense of things, the world would be enhanced; instead of denying humans the desire to explore the unknown, the world would be available for exploration for the first time. It would become the paradise unknown rather than the world after death; it would more than satisfy the "adventurer" in humanity simply because it has never yet truly been seen for what it is. And for Stevens "This is the thesis scrivened in delight, / The reverberating psalm, the right chorale." The "thesis" of a physical people in a physical world would still require forms, but the forms would be "scrivened in delight" rather than written out of despair, and the "reverberating psalm" and the "right chorale" would celebrate this world rather than the prospect of some future one. The joyful aesthetic would not disappear but rather become fully integrated into our way of seeing the world for the first time. Our pain would not disappear, nor would human evil, nor mortality or temporality or bodily functions or anything else; but we would be capable of appreciating these things as they should be appreciated and would be able to celebrate the world we have rather than deny it.

Fittingly, Stevens ends his lengthy exploration of his new aesthetic with celebration, but a celebration that includes everything rather than one that forces the negative aspects of existence off the stage at the end:

> One might have thought of sight, but who could think
>
> Of what it sees, for all the ill it sees?

> Speech found the ear, for all the evil sound,
> But the dark italics it could not propound.
> And out of what one sees and hears and out
> Of what one feels, who could have thought to make
> So many selves, so many sensuous worlds,
> As if the air, the mid-day air, was swarming
> With the metaphysical changes that occur,
> Merely in living as and where we live.

Stevens chose an aural rather than a visual metaphor for his aesthetic because vision is so easily overwhelmed by the evil of the world. It sees so much "ill" that it seems to find no way of getting beyond it. Speech, on the other hand, in spite of the "evil sound" that the world contains, "found the ear," was capable of appreciating and articulating the harmony of the world even in the presence of evil. But until now, speech "could not propound" "the dark italics." The darker side of the world has not been adequately addressed by speech because it was devoted to writing over and ignoring the "dark italics." They never really disappeared, but we could at least imagine a "chorale" that had only pleasing notes. Stevens' chorale, however, is an "Esthétique du *Mal*," so it includes the dark italics as part of the measure of the pleasing notes. It hits *all* of the notes and refuses to leave out the seemingly discordant ones.

Among all of the notes of the chorale one finds a place for amazement, a spot where the daily business of life is transformed and one is awed by the fact that "out of what one sees and hears and out / Of what one feels" "So many selves, so many sensuous worlds" appear of which one was previously unaware. Instead of finding that the world is reduced when it is seen as completely physical, we see that it is expanded. Instead of being circumscribed by a single self and a single world, we discover many selves and many sensuous worlds, opening up rather than closing down future possibilities. We no longer need to imagine a metaphysical world that will generate vast transformations in our being because "the mid-day air" is "swarming" with the equivalent of metaphysical changes, and these transformations come about "Merely in living as and where we live." There is no need for another world because this one finally comes to be seen as sufficient for our desires. It doesn't eliminate desire—which we think we want—but it affords more than enough unknown possibilities for us to explore and fulfill our sense of achievement.

Of course, this "paradise unknown" is indeed still largely unknown. Humans have yet fully to see the value inherent in it, just as they have been unwilling to face those things that Stevens' aesthetic would force them to see. But our present inability to accept this vision does not take away its value; it still provides us with the possibilities we think we want, and it still offers a full account of both the good and the evil of the world, the joy and the pain, and as such it remains the most comprehensive vision we have. The only question in the end is whether or not humans have the strength and courage to become "wholly human," are capable of conceiving of a race "Completely physical in a physical world." Stevens has provided us with a perspective that we can finally either measure up to or retreat from, and he can do no more than that. If we look at the conclusions Stevens came to in the context of his poetry and his life, we can see that for him too there was great struggle involved in *beginning* to accept the world as it is. As he was no more or less human than we are, he thus demonstrates both the difficulties and the possibilities inherent in his aesthetic and thereby leaves the future open for us to determine.

. . . . . .

When we look at the ethical implications of "Esthétique du Mal," we might get a stronger sense of its value if we consider the kind of poetry Stevens wrote, for in an important way this poem is a striking departure for him. The vast majority of Stevens' work seems devoid of the natural world, and it has precious little to say about human relationships or human emotion. Stevens seems much more of an intellectual poet, and when we think of a writer who bases his work on an interest in the natural world, certainly someone like Williams comes to mind a long time before Stevens ever does. It was Stevens, after all, who was prone to exclaim (and lament): "It is a world of words to the end of it." Likewise, Stevens was much more locked into the nineteenth-century obsession with the relationship between self and other, self and world, as we see even in a poem like "Esthétique." Williams begins with a set of assumptions that denies the value of the self/other difference from the outset; he sees himself in the scene and feels no need to recover a lost unity.

Similarly, Stevens' work doesn't concern itself much with the value of love any more than it seriously explores the parameters of human emotion. For the most part it confines itself to never-ending articulations of the question of reality, self and language, and other people seldom enter in. Without the occasional poem like "Esthétique," it might seem as though Stevens had absolutely no interest in anything other than a purely intellectual poetry, devoted to the connections that exist between self, language and world. The biographical facts of Stevens' life also contribute to a vision of him as someone who was rather remote, detached from the natural world and the exuberance that someone like Williams found in it. His interests seem more akin to the symbolist tendencies in his poetry: he loves the refined sophistication of a Japanese print or some other precious object much more than he delights in the odor of a rose or the sight of a beautiful sunset.

Stevens, then, seems the last person we would expect to tell us that "the greatest poverty is not to live in a physical world" simply because he doesn't seem to live in a physical world. And yet in "Esthétique du Mal" that is precisely what he says, just as he turns to the value of human love in this poem, in contrast to most of his other work. Inasmuch as this is a relatively late poem, we can assume that Stevens makes this statement on the basis of experience, either negative—he now realizes what he has missed by ignoring the physical world—or positive—he has finally seen how a commitment to the physical world is the ground of a valuable life. Either way, the aesthetic that is articulated in "Esthétique" remains the fullest expression of Stevens' vision, even if the poems that follow it are, like the ones before, often committed to elaborations of the question of reality and our ability to know it.

The ethical implications of the poem should be quite clear by now, for one can hardly discuss the world presented in the poem without demonstrating the ways in which it suggests an ethical vision of life. As with Whitman or any other great poet, Stevens does not tell us how to live. He simply presents an aesthetic vision that has a way of life built into it. When he tells us that "The greatest poverty is not to live in a physical world," we must see that as a statement of value. If the greatest poverty—and hence the worst way to exist—is not to live in a physical world, then the best life would by definition be one that was based on the physical world. Stevens also carefully qualifies his definition of "physical world" here by saying "a" physical world rather than "the" physical world, for he doesn't want to give the impression that "the real" physical world can ever be definitively known. That issue is less important in this poem than the question of whether one lives in a physical world or denies that world, and from that beginning all the ethical implications of the poem manifest themselves.

In a poem specifically devoted to the question of pain and evil, we would naturally expect there to be extensive discussion of what evil is and how it affects the value of our lives, and "Esthétique" provides that. Instead of locating the "mal" of the world in some external or otherwordly source, and instead of attributing it to our bodies and animal characteristics, Stevens repeatedly shows that evil is inherent in humanity itself. There is nothing terribly striking about that; after all, that is what Christianity teaches as well. But Stevens doesn't place the evil in the body or the bodily functions any more than he attributes it to original sin. It is simply a function of our finitude and the related desire to escape a world in which "to be is not enough to be." These factors generate the vengefulness that accounts for most of the evil in the world, and Stevens shows how they work at the individual and social levels. Pain, however, is not evil per se; it is something we experience as a result of being alive, and it is not a function of our vengefulness, even if our desire for revenge does have built into it the belief that we can eliminate pain as well as evil from our lives. But Stevens simply asserts that "Pain is human," and there is little else to be said. It must be accepted as a part of life and cannot be denied.

The factor that most affects the way we view pain is our self-centeredness: because we feel that pain ought not to be part of ordinary life, believing it to be a kind of punishment meted out for those who are evil, we take the pain we experience personally and become resentful of the world itself because it forces us to live through pain as well as joy. The world's indifference to our pain makes us feel alienated and ill-dealt with, so we eventually use it to justify our desires to deny the world too. But if it is simply a function of being alive, there is no reason to take pain personally, and if it is nothing personal, there is no reason to become resentful because we are forced to experience it.

The crucial aspects of Stevens' vision inevitably come back to questions of value. In contrast to a mode that he finds essentially negative and life-denying, Stevens time and again asserts the positive value of accepting what we are and what the world is. In contrast to a mode that argues the world is primarily an evil and corrupt place, Stevens argues that the world is chiefly neither evil nor good. It just is, and we are the ones who make it evil or good. In contrast to a mode that places the beauty and the joy of life into an after-world as a compensation for the pain and evil of this one, Stevens asserts that the world we live in is fundamentally beautiful and harmonious. In terms of the traditional perspective, the problem with the harmonies of the world is simply that they include pain and evil as well as joy and the good, and rather than choosing to live within those harmonies, we prefer to deny the evil. The result, however, is that we also end up denying the good, and this is why Stevens finds the greatest poverty in the individual who doesn't live in a physical world. Such a person hasn't really eliminated the pain and evil of life. He has found an explanation for it that seems to justify its presence in his daily life, and he has a hypothetical compensation for it in the dream of an afterlife, but he has paid for this "understanding" with alienation and has lost the beauty of this world at the same time.

Equally important when it comes to the question of value, the traditional denial of evil and negation of life serve to perpetuate precisely that which one hopes to avoid. Instead of eliminating evil, this perspective reinforces it by projecting it elsewhere and by choosing a way of life that makes it impossible to discern the vengefulness at the heart of one's own choices. So one ends up sacrificing the beauty of this world for the prospect of a better world later, and one also guarantees that this world will not get any better but will only continue to be driven by the same desires for retribution and recompense. The negation of value in this way of life saturates everything, even if the denials themselves seem virtuous and the exponents of such a view proclaim their lives good. In the end they deny the value of life, and insofar as they do, their values remain negative.

Again, Stevens' aesthetic tells no one precisely what values to have. It only articulates the fundamentals upon which one's values can be based. It assumes that one's values can be positive only if one accepts what is rather than seeks to build something impossible, but Stevens also makes it clear that the task he sets before us is a most difficult one: we have yet to become wholly human or to imagine a "race / Completely physical in a physical world" because it has always been easier to imagine ourselves as non-physical people who hoped for a non-physical world. The older view offers "sleek ensolacings" that are all too tempting. Humans value greatly the idea that everything should make sense, and so any vision that can *explain* why there is pain and evil comforts them because the words themselves are soothing. And when the explanation also offers the prospect of escaping from everything about this world that they don't like, it becomes almost too seductive. Perhaps, indeed, humans are finally incapable of accepting their humanity. Perhaps they can live only through the feeble illusion that they understand. The "as ifs" and "it seems" of the poem certainly demonstrate that Stevens could be no more sure of the possibility for human change—even in his own life—than anyone else could be. But at the very least the aesthetic vision compensates for the loss of the "sleek ensolacings" by returning the beauty of the world to us, and by making it easier for us to live with ourselves. And if one could assume that this makes the trade-off even (and of course one *cannot* assume this), one might also be tempted to believe that it is possible for us to become wholly human, for the Stevensian view has one more valuable component: it reflects the preponderant evidence we have of what the world truly is like. It is based upon what we all more or less know to be true at some level, and if we do indeed have some desire to know the world as it is—or to get as close to that as we can—then this greater accuracy alone ought to tip the scales in favor of Stevens' vision.

In the end, these questions of efficacy are beyond the scope of the poem and have nothing to do with Stevens' job as a poet. His function is simply to articulate the world as clearly as he can, and that he has done. We can expect no more of him than that. Then the expectations return to us and what we are capable of. We can ignore Stevens' aesthetic and choose instead the two most obvious alternatives: the all-too-easy and fashionable pessimism that revels in a view of the world as a degraded and hopeless place, or the equally easy Romanticism that simply prefers to escape from the degradations of the world via a nostalgic aesthetic of rarefied flowers and cloistered rooms. Both visions are finally pessimistic, of course; they simply reflect two responses to the pessimistic possibilities. One can also view Stevens' work in one of these two ways and eliminate the complex rigors of his aesthetic, and his poetry is often construed from precisely these angles. But if one begins with "Esthétique du Mal" as the consummate expression of Stevens' values, one inevitably comes to the conclusion that his vision is the most adventurous of all, and that the difficulties inherent in embracing it are compensated for by the beauties to which it returns us.

Chapter Three

AMMONS AND THE ONE: MANY MECHANISM

In the contemporary period, there are any number of poets whose work has a specifically ethical component to it, but no one has a more comprehensive vision of the relationship between his aesthetic and the ethics that are implicit in it than A. R. Ammons. Inasmuch as he is clearly in the Whitmanian tradition, we should not be surprised to find this to be so, but even given his heritage, the striking thing about Ammons' work is how fully it manages to delineate the world and all of its implications without resorting to a nostalgia for an older vision. If Stevens convinces us in "Esthétique du Mal" that the greatest poverty is not to live in a physical world, and if he is thorough in his articulation of a physical world, in the overall context of his work we must see him as someone who was not totally able to separate himself from his nineteenth-century heritage. He still couches his statements in terms of the "as if" and the "seems," uncertain of whether others can measure up to his vision, uncertain if even he can measure up to it.

Ammons, on the other hand, like Williams, *begins* with the world Stevens ends up with. He does not devote his poetry to the question of whether his vision is realizable—it already exists, and so that point has been put to rest. The difficulties inherent in his vision are the same ones in Stevens' or Whitman's work, and Ammons makes a point of showing them to us, but he develops a poetic voice that seldom questions the viability of the aesthetic. This shift toward accepting what *is* as a beginning premise rather than a final one makes it possible for Ammons to work through more fully the various elements of his perspective and allows him to measure out the world in ways that Stevens never could. Put another way, we can say that in Ammons' poetry we do get a sense of the natural world, and, as with Williams, we get a sense of the speaker in the poem being out in that world. In

Stevens we only find continual approaches to the world itself, and never feel confident that the speaker of a poem really is in the midst of the physical world toward which his thoughts are directed. The speaker in Ammons' poems articulates his thoughts in the midst of the world rather than using them to arrive there, and as such they are natural outgrowths of the world rather than attempts to achieve a rapprochement with it.

Although the particular feel of the natural world in Ammons' work is probably best felt in a classic poem like "Corsons Inlet," the theoretical underpinnings of that work are best explored in a longer poem like "Essay on Poetics," where the same process is operative but is designed to flesh out the value of poetry and the world. And if we could say that one of the reasons Stevens tended only to approach the physical world rather than actually arrive at it was that he was skeptical of language's capabilities, we can see how Ammons dispenses with Stevens' difficulties at the very beginning. Instead of being overly preoccupied with the question of whether or not our language and forms prevent us from experiencing the world, Ammons shows how these forms, while artificial, do nothing to cut us off from the world of which we are a part:

> Take in a lyric information
> totally processed, interpenetrated into
> wholeness where
>
> a bit is a bit, a string a string, a
> cluster a cluster, everything beefing up
> and verging out
>
> for that point in the periphery where
> salience bends into curve
> and all saliences bend to the same angle of
>
> curve and curve becomes curve, one curve, the whole curve:
> that is information actual
> at every point

but taking on itself at every point
the emanation of curvature, of meaning, all
the way into the high

recognition of wholeness, that synthesis,
feeling, aroused, controlled, and released:
but then find the wholeness

unbelievable because it permits
another wholeness,
another lyric, the same in structure . . .[1]

In a "lyric information" that is "totally processed" everything has "interpenetrated into / wholeness," as one would expect inasmuch as unity is supposed to be one of the primary components of all poems. But this wholeness allows a "bit" to be a bit, a "string" to be a string. It hasn't sacrificed the particulars to the "curve" of meaning into which all these bits enter. The particulars are changed as "curve becomes curve, one curve, the whole curve," but they still remain discrete. As Ammons puts it, they remain "information actual" even as they have taken on "at every point / the emanation of curvature, of meaning."

Given the swings of Ammons' poems, though, the curvature of these particulars has no sooner reached the "high / recognition of wholeness" with the "feeling" "aroused, controlled, and released," than it recognizes that this wholeness is "unbelievable because it permits / another wholeness, / another lyric, the same in structure." Even more, this other lyric will bear a "different weight" and might have a "perhaps contradicting . . . bit-nature and assimilation" (30,31). Inasmuch as the one lyric "permits / another wholeness," it could hardly be said to be all-encompassing, and inasmuch as the other lyric might well contradict it in its particulars and would have a different meaning, one immediately confronts the problem of language and form. If one completed form can be contradicted by another; if one wholeness doesn't totally correspond to another wholeness; of what value is the word "wholeness"? The tacit admission is that there is no such thing as wholeness, at least as it is traditionally defined. Every "wholeness" is at best a partial wholeness, and thus not really a wholeness at all. And if the wholeness that our language and forms gives us is partial at best, then we must assume that it is faulty, reductive, illusory, or at least that is what we traditionally have thought.

But Ammons establishes his own ground by quickly dealing with this problem of form when he tells us that

> wholeness then is a condition of existence,
>
> a one:many mechanism, internally irrelevant to scope,
>
> but from the outside circumscribed into scope. . . . (31)

These three lines articulate the basic genius of Ammons' perspective and fully account for its confidence. He begins by assuming that wholeness "is a condition of existence." Instead of arguing that for humans wholeness is something to be achieved—and perhaps only rarely—Ammons tells us that it is an essential element of our being in the world. Wholeness exists even if we are not always able to perceive it. The problem, then, is not in achieving wholeness but in recognizing that we *already have it,* not in reintegrating ourselves into the world but in seeing how we are already inevitably integrated simply because we exist. We are part of the "one:many mechanism" that is the fundamental condition of all living things. And if we are part of this mechanism by dint of being alive, there is no need to find ourselves within it—we are already there and always have been.

Our understanding of language and form, though, suggests that we are removed from the world, and our symbolic systems demonstrate this because they are at best partial formulations of what is. Ammons responds that the one:many mechanism is "internally irrelevant to scope, / but from the outside circumscribed into scope." Any particular "wholeness" finds scope to be irrelevant if it truly is a wholeness—that is, a form that contains both the bits of life and their curvature—simply because it reveals the one:many mechanism that is at the heart of life. If that one:many mechanism has both the one and the many, then it has wholeness even if it doesn't include everything in its oneness or its manyness. Equally built into this statement is the awareness that *all* wholeness is thus limited, appearing whole within its domain but being "circumscribed into scope" from "the outside." With this knowledge one can see both how wholeness exists within a limited scope just as one discerns that it can *only* exist within a limited scope, always suggesting yet other ways the one:many mechanism can be circumscribed.

The problem that Ammons is essentially dispensing with here is the one that has bedeviled the twentieth century more than any other, and it has found its formulation in virtually every discipline. The problem of sets as Gödel established it, for example, was that one set always depends on another, more comprehensive set for its premises; as a result, the set of all sets is a contradiction, for no matter how large the scope of one set, it will always depend upon premises outside of it. We find this problem inherent in the law of non-contradiction, in the question of cultural relativity, in the interpretation of poems, and everywhere else. And in most cases the result of this problem has been an endless preoccupation with the ways we are deceived by our desire for totality and our total inability ever to achieve it.

Ammons doesn't solve the problem, of course, for it cannot be solved. He simply declares it irrelevant *so long as one is aware of the limits of the wholeness one articulates.* There is no point in worrying the problem of the set of all sets to death, for it will always remain as a reflection of the limits of human understanding. So, one begins with the awareness of this limit and then proceeds to see the kinds of "truth" that are available within the circumscribed vision we always inevitably have. The boundary is important because it does circumscribe things, but it is not so important that we should devote our energies to endlessly circulating around its perimeter. It is more important to see the way the one:many mechanism works within a series of limits, and that is precisely what Ammons' poems do.

Having established what he is *not* going to worry about—whether his poem is complete and totalized and whole in the idealist sense—Ammons proceeds to show us via example why he is not concerned with the final order, and he does so through a deliberately artificial choice: "I like the order that allows, say, when / a thousand cows are on a thousand acres . . ." (31). Obviously there is no essential reason why one ought to imagine precisely 1,000 cows on a 1,000 acres—nature itself is never that clearly rounded off, so the number represents an arbitrary choice. But it is not totally arbitrary; it is nicely in the middle. If there were only one cow on one acre, the "natural" sampling would be too small to make significant statements about. Every fact would reflect with certainty only the behavior of one cow, which would mean that one could not decide if its patterns were typical or idiosyncratic. Likewise, 10,000 cows would give much more information that 1,000 cows, but they would give *too much* information, and the extra 9,000 cows would not add significantly to the knowledge of "cow pattern" that the poet would seek. So 1,000 cows is large enough for Ammons to be able to discern the curve of cow pattern, but small enough for him to be able to manage. The number is both arbitrary and capable of generating statements of provisional truth.

But what kinds of statements could a poet make about 1,000 cows that would be the least bit interesting? Ammons explains:

> . . . after a while I could account for the motions of
>
> the whole herd and make interesting statements:
> for example, with experience, I bet I could tell
> from the wear under a copse
>
> whether a lot of hot sunny days in a year
> or windy days come: I could tell something obvious already
> from the copse whether it constitutes a meaningful
>
> windbreak in a cold wind, sand or snow storm, and then
> that, though obvious, would tell about cows. . . . (31)

We might not need to know these things about cows that the poet could tell us if he were observing 1,000 of them, but he clearly could learn a great deal about both the cows and the environment of which they were a part. And even if we weren't interested in the cows themselves, what he would learn would show us a great deal about natural patterns, about the way organisms within fields accommodate the local environment to themselves and vice versa. The curve of meaning of the cows would thus also elaborate on the curve of meaning inherent in the natural patterns of which we too are a part.

The use of language and arbitrary pattern in the example of the cows demonstrates why Ammons feel he can articulate the truth even if his means are artificial, and he is quick to claim that he is not making up illusory patterns with his artificial structure. As he tells us: "the way I think is / I think what I see:the designs are there:I use / words to draw them out . . ." (32). The form through which things are understood might be artificial, but the patterns that emerge are not simply imposed upon the natural world by the poet. On the contrary, he thinks "what he see[s]:the designs are there." He may "use / words to draw them out," but the designs exist outside of his perception of them. There is truth value to the poet's statements, then, in spite of the fact that the means used to achieve them are "unnatural" and artificial. The patterns themselves are all part of the one:many mechanism that exists outside of and within the language that we use. It is not something we construct in order to fulfill our desire for wholeness, and it is not an illusion.

If the patterns of nature exist before the poet's articulation of them, though, the problem of verification remains, and this is a problem only because language itself is part of the process it seeks to articulate. Thus, one cannot simply pick apart the poet's words one at a time to discern their truth value; they must be seen as a part of a pattern just as the cows on the land must be seen as part of a pattern:

> stop on any word and language gives way:
>
> the blades of reason, unlightened by motion, sink in,
>
> melting through, and reality's cold murky waters
>
> accept the failure. . . . (32)

Dissecting the particular words with the "blades of reason" does not reveal the truth of the statements. On the contrary, it forces language to give way, and everything grinds to a halt. Truth value does not inhere in any particular word any more than it inheres in any particular cow, for words no more exist in isolation than cows do. One can only discern their value through the articulation of their pattern. With cows this is easy to see, but it is less visible with language because we have accustomed ourselves to investigating it word by word. This procedure for determining the efficacy of statements, however, was developed at a time when it was thought that words had representational meaning, when we believed that they pointed to things in the external world. Ammons recognizes that words aren't representational; again, their value inheres in their pattern and not in the things to which they refer, for language is admittedly an artificial medium.

Ammons explains the way that language works in the following way:

> . . . language heightens by dismissing reality,
>
> the sheet of ice a salience controlling, like a symbol,

> level of abstraction, that has a hold on reality and suppresses
> it, though formed from it and supported by it:
>
> motion and artificiality (the impositional remove from reality)
> sustain language: nevertheless, language must
> not violate the bit, the event, percept,
>
> fact—the concrete—otherwise the separation that means
> the death of language shows: when that happens abandonment
> is the only terrible health and a return to bits, re-trials
>
> of lofty configurations. . . . (32,33)

Because "language heightens by dismissing reality," one cannot expect of it a literal representation of the way things are; that is not its business. It is, however, "formed from [reality] and supported by it." It is not something that is devoid of that out of which the patterns of the world are elaborated, and its own patterns are supported by those of the natural world. At the same time, "motion and artificiality (the impositional remove from reality) / sustain language." It cannot compete with "reality" because it is more (and less) than reality per se. It can only arrive at statements of value through a deliberate removal from reality and through the imposition of an artificial form.

Language reduces by abstracting from the world, framing the information it contains and leaving things out, but at the same time it "must / not violate the bit, event, percept, / fact—the concrete." It must be based upon "bits" and "events," the concrete facts of our everyday lives, and it cannot violate these facts without losing its validity. Once its bits violate the bits of reality, "the separation that means / the death of language shows." The bits of language can be measured in terms of the bits of reality from which they were derived, and if they fail to uphold that measure, language fails. This, after all, is the way through which we test the truth of statements; we compare them to what we know and what is, and if they don't correspond either to what we know or to what is, we are forced to conclude that "abandonment / is the only terrible health and a return to bits, re-trials." If the statements don't adhere to the bits of the world, then even if we are enamored of the words themselves, we must abandon them and start over, going back to the bits and trying again to ascertain their truth value. We can always ignore the fact that our statements don't apply to reality and choose instead to live within the illusion they create, but anyone truly interested in preserving language and developing an accurate sense of the world would prefer to abandon his cherished statements and return to the world to build a new series of patterns to articulate the world.

In a general way Ammons' statements deal with the problem of language in a neat and simple way: they circumscribe its limits and proceed within them. They eliminate the need to be endlessly preoccupied with the artificiality of language at the same time that they remind us of the need always to test our statements against the world from which they were derived. In this way, Ammons manages to maintain his confidence in language at the same time that he is suspicious of it, and he also reasserts our ability to know the world as a result. But there is another problem hidden within the question of the validity of language, and it concerns the ground upon which all truth is supposed to be based. In arguing that if we "stop on any word . . . language gives way," Ammons has removed the grounds for establishing with certitude its truth. The ground of things cannot be located in language, which would not be a problem if it weren't for the fact that neither the external world nor the world of the self can provide a ground either. Ammons is literally arguing for a groundless truth, yet another contradiction of our traditional ways of conceiving of things, and he demonstrates the way he deals with this problem by telling us that

> a center's absolute, if relative: but every point is spacetimematter's
>
> a center: reality is abob with centers: indeed, there is
> nothing but centers: centers of galaxies, systems, planets, asteroids,
> moons, drifts, atoms, electrons: and the center, as of the
>
> earth, where all turns and pressures meet, is inexpressibly light,
> still, and empty. . . . (33)

A center—to be a center in the traditional conception—must be absolute, and Ammons concedes that it is; but he also maintains that it is relative at the same time. It is absolute from its own perspective but relative from any other location in the world. So there is a center, but there really isn't at the same time. After all, if there is a center, there ought to be only *one* center, and Ammons claims that "every point is spacetimematter's / a center: reality is abob with centers." If everything is a center, then nothing is really a center, at least as we used to think of these things. We are always centered in a particular way because we are a point in spacetimematter, but inasmuch as there are countless other points, our absoluteness is severely undermined. And if our point in spacetimematter is undercut in this way, so too is every other one, including the most obvious of grounds, the earth, which, while it is the point "where all turns and pressures meet," is nevertheless "inexpressibly light, / still, and empty."

These troubling violations of the law of non-contradiction don't bother Ammons at all; for him they simply express the way things are and explain why language has truth value even if it is artificial, why we can determine the truth from our own particular point in spacetimematter at the same time that we must always be measuring that truth from other points in spacetimematter as best as we can. Instead of finding hard ground at the center of these processes, Ammons finds the "inexpressibly light, / still and empty" force that is life itself, but he is not bothered by its lack of substantiality. That it is still and empty does not eliminate its value; it simply forces us radically to reconceive our ways of thinking about life and our relation to everything that is. And just to make sure that we've gotten the point, Ammons also turns to the lyric poem itself, that linguistic creation that has for centuries been thought to deliver the true presence of things to us. The lyric, we are told, "has never been found out because at the center it, too, is / empty, still, silent . . ." (34). The lyric poem "has never been found out" because it is no more substantial than anything else in the world. If it were, the final lyric poem would have already been written, and there would be no need for any more. But its silence reflects the silence at the center of life itself, and as such it must always be described again and again. Only something that was grounded could be finally established, and if our world were built in that way, its end point would be determinable. Fortunately, it is not.

If the world is based on stillness and emptiness, and if all centers are absolute but relative, the means through which our understanding of this stillness is developed need to be determined, and once again Ammons goes about doing this in a way that thoroughly undermines our traditional conception of things. He reminds us that the "main confluence" of his poem is "one:many" and then tells us how he goes about exploring the one:many:

> . . . I get lost for fun,
>
> because there's no chance of getting lost: I am seeking the
> mechanisms physical, physiological, epistemological, electrical
>
> chemical, esthetic, social, religious, by which many, kept
> discrete as many, expresses itself into the
> manageable rafters of salience. . . . (34)

Ammons claims he "get[s] lost for fun, / because there's no chance of getting lost," and this seems to be a description of his method. He chooses deliberately to get lost, to give up self-conscious control of his thoughts, and allows himself to be led by whatever comes to him, whether it be something that he thinks of or something from the external world that stimulates him. And while he uses the rather glib word "fun" here, quite clearly he is referring to that which used to be characterized by joy, as we shall see in a moment. The aesthetic vision upon which Ammons' poems are based, then, derives from his willingness to forego his desire for control and structure, depends on his ability to let things happen as they will. Most of us prefer to be in control, to know where we're going and why, so we are unlikely to pursue this course because it seems to leave us too vulnerable, too susceptible to the whims of the external world. But Ammons informs us that he gets lost "because there's no chance of getting lost." Our greatest fear of letting go is that we shall get lost in some way and won't be able to find our way back; Ammons maintains that when one decides to get lost for fun, there's no chance of getting lost, presumably because one finds oneself amidst the patterns of the world of which one is always a part anyway. Hence, he is not at all troubled by the suspension of his desire for control, realizing that only by leaving it behind will he be able to find what he wants to find.

Ammons' goal in getting lost is to discern the "mechanisms physical, physiological, epistemological, electrical, / chemical, esthetic, social, religious" that provide our world with its patterns of understanding. He is not simply concerned with aesthetic beauty or joy, nor is his interest primarily philosophical truth. He wants to discern the patterns underlying all of the major human domains, whether they be physical, social or natural. And he can seek all of these patterns because they are not discrete fields in themselves; they all have similarities that help further to reveal their own curve of meaning and articulate the one:many mechanism at the same time. Implicitly, then, the poet can begin with any one of these mechanisms and discern some of the parameters of the others simply by tracing out the lines to their points of connection. And when this happens, the many "expresses itself into the / manageable rafters of salience," illuminates the larger patterns that strike one with their truth value and their beauty. Indeed, Ammons is so impressed by these moments of confluence that he is not content simply to characterize them as occasions that generate "manageable rafters of salience." He himself gets carried away with other ways of expressing the same thing, telling us that the many

> . . . lofts to comprehension, breaks
>
> out in hard, highly informed suasions, the "gathering
> in the sky" so to speak, the trove of mind, tested
> experience, the only place there is to stay, where the saints
>
> are known to share accord and wine, and magical humor floats
> upon the ambient sorrow. . . . (34)

In part Ammons is having fun here with his various explanations of what happens when the many becomes a curve of meaning, but he is also intent on showing us with force that what he is speaking of reveals major patterns and generates one of the chief joys of life: that moment when things come together for us and the world's patterns do indeed seem to make sense. True to his vision, Ammons tells us that "much is nearly stable there" rather than "everything," for there is no place of stability in the world. But during such moments there is enough stability for us to be able to see the way the patterns of which we are a part come together, and hence enough solidity for us to be able to derive a sense of what is true and what is not, what violates the bits of existence and what confirms them. This is what aesthetic experience finally is, regardless of whether it occurs in a poem or in an everyday event, and Ammons does not want to separate the moments of poetic joy from those of everyday life. After all, many poetic experiences emanate from everyday life and return to it, so there is no reason to put the beauty of poetry into a discrete category. If we did so, we would then be incapable of discerning its relation to all those other mechanisms that Ammons is interested in seeking out.

The method of Ammons' poem is perfectly suited to his means, and it is just as fitting to a late-twentieth-century sense of the world. At the same time, the poet's procedure is as old as humankind and as simple as it possibly could be: "hue a middle way, the voice / replied, which is what I'm doing the best I can . . ." (36). For Ammons hueing a middle way means simply this: "I proceed a little way into similarity and / withdraw a bit into differentiae. . . ." If he goes too far into similarity, the bits of reality are violated and truth value is lost; if he goes too far into differentiae, the curve of meaning is lost and truth value once again disappears. This is perhaps not the ideal mode of knowledge—and perhaps not the one we might have wished for—but, as Ammons says, "unfortunately, man cannot / do better though it might be better done." It is possible to imagine an epistemological mode that would be devoid of the flaws of the simple hueing of a middle way, a tricky business that is difficult to learn and hard to maintain, but it is not possible for humans to do things any better than this, so rather than imagining other possibilities, Ammons chooses to work within the limits that human nature sets for him.

The dangers of the middle way should be obvious. We tend to forget ourselves too easily and lean one way or the other, overwhelming the bits of the world with our speculations about them, forever covering them up with the crude and illusory artifice we construct in the process, or we immerse ourselves so thoroughly into the bits of the world that we forget altogether that there is indeed pattern to be found within the relations among them, pattern that is both necessary for our understanding of the world and capable of providing us with the joy that comes from perceiving the inherent beauty of the world. One must be eternally vigilant to keep up the process of the middle way, and it may be the hardest thing for humans to do.

Even more, it could be said that Ammons' easy dismissal of other possibilities is a bit too hasty and glib, gliding over the very real problems with his own method. He too admits to being troubled by his procedures, but he maintains that there is simply no other way humans can go about learning of the world. One of the examples that he uses to explore the necessity for his method is a poem about an elm tree, which is once again both a flippant and a totally serious account of the difficulties in thinking and writing about anything. In order to understand the elm tree, Ammons has to know a great deal about it: what kind of tree it is, where it's located, what systems it feeds into and out of, what larger patterns it is a part of, and so on. He can easily enough determine some of these, but, for example, when it comes to locating precisely the tree about which he is writing, he can quickly become bogged down in hopeless difficulties:

> I ought to know the altitude, then, from some fixed point:
> I assume the fixed point would have to be
>   the core center of the planet, though I'm perfectly
> prepared to admit the core's involved
>   in a slow—perhaps universal—slosh that would alter the
>   center's position
> in terms of some other set of references I do not
> think I will at the moment entertain
> since to do so invites an outward, expanding
> reticulation
> too much to deal precisely with:
>
> true, I really ought to know where the tree is: but I know
> it's in my backyard:
> I've never found it anywhere else and am willing to accept the
>   precision of broadness: with over-precision
> things tend to fade. . . . (38)

If he wants to be as specific as possible about the location of the tree, he will exhaust great amounts of time trying to pin it down, and even then he will have had to assume certain arbitrary conventions. Even if he can locate it in terms of the core of the earth, he will have to ignore the fact that the core of the earth is also moving; hence his measurements will be imprecise. Our instruments have become so sophisticated that there always seems to be another level of precision that is possible to achieve, and while this precision is useful at times, for the poet's enterprise it would be too much. So Ammons says "true, I really ought to know where the tree is: but I know it's in my backyard," and that is sufficiently precise for his purposes. After all, he's never found it anywhere else" and so he is "willing to accept the precision of broadness":

> I am just going to take it for granted
> that the tree is in the backyard:
> it's necessary to be quiet in the hands of the marvelous. . . . (39)

As with the thousand cows, the limit of the tree's location as his backyard is artificial, but it will allow him to arrive at the understanding he desires, and by avoiding the needless precision that is available to him he is able to "be quiet in the hands of the marvelous" and recognize the wonder that the tree embodies. If he got bogged down in detail, he would lose the sense of the marvelous.

Even if the poet accepts the precision of broadness, though, there is still far more for him to observe than he can ever duly note. If he is interested in "the gradualism of sway, / of growth's sway," the processes are so intricate that he can only hope to gather the largest features. He must attend to the effect of humans on the tree, in this case the way in which his son's swing affects the bottom limb; he must pay attention to the changes that are wrought by the growth of the leaves, by the effects of the wind and sun, by the sinking of the earth; he must note the ways in which the elmworm both lightens the tree by eating part of it and opens it up for further growth in the process; and each of these things must be seen in relation to one another, for they all compose the environment that the tree is and lives within. And even if he manages to do all this, he will have only inscribed the most obvious features of the elm tree, though what he perceives will be sufficient to give a good idea of what the tree is and how it fits into the world.

The middle way, then, requires both "broad awareness" and attention to detail, and the dialectic between the two makes understanding possible, even if at the limits both individual perspectives are flawed:

> broad awareness is the gift of settle minds: or of
> minds hurt high from painful immediacy: it eliminates
> and jettisons
> sensory contact with too much accident and event—total
>   dependencies at the edge: the man
> fully aware,
> unable to separate out certain large motions, probably
> couldn't move: it's better, I think, to be
> broadly and emptily aware so as more efficiently
> to negotiate the noons of recurrence. . . . (40)

One who simply attended to his senses "probably / couldn't move" because he would be unable to detect pattern and would be overwhelmed by information. One who is "broadly and emptily aware" can more efficiently "negotiate the noons of recurrence" and recognize the patterns that emerge from the repetition of experience.

When the noons of recurrence can be discerned and placed into patterns, one must also be aware of a corollary problem:

> one thing
>
> always to keep in mind is that there are a number of possibilities:
>
> whatever sways forward implies a backward sway and the mind must
> either go all the way around and come back or it must be prepared
> to fall back and deal with the lost sway, the pressure for dealing
>
> increasing constantly with forwardness. . . . (43)

Because we tend to have linear conceptions of the world, and because those conceptions tend to get easily reinforced by the noons of recurrence, we forget that "whatever sways forward implies a backward sway." We then lose sight of the sway altogether, and that is precisely what we need to remember, for only it is capable of revealing pattern and establishing the ways in which the forward and backward movement of things generates the patterns of life. We usually read the world from ourselves outward, for example, forgetting that we need also to read from the world back to ourselves, and the same dialectic applies to every process we observe. If the sway is lost, objects and subjects become reified, and that means we lose our sense of the aesthetic of the world.

. . . . . .

The job of the poet is to present us with the broad awareness of the double sway of the world, and he can do so only because poems too are part of that sway rather than mere commentaries about it. Indeed, Ammons goes so far as to suggest that

> . . . poems, of human make, are
>
> body images, organisms of this human organism: if that isn't

> so I will be terribly disappointed: it sounds as if it ought to
> be right: consonants, vowels, idioms, phrases, clauses (tissues),
>
> sentences (organs), verses (organ systems), poems (living worlds):
> I react to such stuff with a burst of assent resembling for all
> I can tell valuable feeling. . . . (47)

In its own way this is nothing more than an updated version of the organic metaphor, and while there is a certain amount of truth to it, the correspondences in the patterns are such that one cannot take them too seriously. One may well "react to such stuff with a burst of assent," but the pattern has value only so long as one remembers the *difference* hidden in it as well. Poems are in a real way "organisms of this human organism," but at the same time their tissue is not really alive as human tissue is; they are part of the world—and certainly part of our world—but their existence is different in kind than ours, even if the patterns do make some sense out of the way poetry works and even if they explain why poems are capable of articulating the world in spite of their artificiality.

What is at the heart of the organic metaphor for Ammons is what he calls the "organizing principle." Human and poetic organisms are both based on the "organizing principle" that gives shape to the systems of the world. True to his "fun" approach in the poem, Ammons tells us that if it is true that the organic metaphor generates a "burst of assent resembling . . . valuable feeling,"

> . . . rubbing a girl also, of course,
>
> produces feeling, I would be the last to deny it, but it may be
> precisely the organization-principle in girls that one, rubbing,
> is pleasured by. . . . (47)

We are not given to thinking that the pleasure we feel in the presence of sexual contact is the result of "the organization-principle in girls" or in boys, but that makes at least as much sense out of the phenomenon as anything else we might imagine. And if both the organic poem and sexual contact participate in the same organization principle, their pattern as well as their joy must be related.

It is hardly new to compare the joy a poem generates to sexual ecstasy, but Ammons has a much broader way of conceiving the analogy; indeed, for him it is much more than analogy—it is a reflection of the basic commonality of the fundamental processes of the world. Here, for example, is his description of how a poem works and what it has in common with the rest of life:

> . . . in poems, the insubstantial processes of becoming
> form inscrutable parts of the living thing: and then how the
>
> orders of the poem build up and cooperate into the pure heat of
> sight and insight, trembling and terror: it makes me gasp aghast:
> no wonder we pedants talk about history, influence, meaning
>
> in poems: that's peripheral enough to prevent the commission of
> larger error, and safe error is a pedantic preference well-known,
> widely footnoted, and amply rewarded: I believe in fun:
>
> "superior amusement" is a little shitty: fun is nice: it's what
> our society is built on: fun in the enterprise: I believe in it:
> I have no faith in the scoffers: they are party-poopers who are
>
> afraid they ought to believe in history or logical positivism and
> don't have any real desire to do so: they are scarcely worth a
> haircut: organisms, I can tell you, build up under the thrust to
>
> joy and nothing else can lift them out of the miry circumstance:
> and poems are pure joy, however divisionally they sway with grief:
> the way to joy is integration's delivery of the complete lode. (47,48)

Ammons asserts that poems have their own "insubstantial processes of becoming" just like any other organism, and these processes "form inscrutable parts of the living thing." These insubstantial processes, in turn, allow the "orders of the poem [to] build up and cooperate into the pure heat of / sight and insight, trembling and terror." The orders combine to generate an ecstatic insight into the overall pattern of things that fills one with sublime trembling and terror because the force of the pattern is so overwhelming. Again, Ammons undercuts the sublimity here by saying "it makes me gasp aghast," using word play to diminish some of the power, but he nonetheless is serious about the way the poem builds to its own kind of climax. And because he finds the whole process so mysterious, he also knows why poems are seldom talked about in the proper way: "We pendants talk about history, influence, meaning / in poems" instead of what the poem is really doing because these concerns are "peripheral enough to prevent the commission of / larger error," mistaking the nature of poetry's sublime processes. In the end, though, poetry's sublimity and its ability to achieve an articulation of the one:many mechanism are what make it valuable.

Ammons is also taking a swipe at academic criticism here, however much he seems to include himself among the "pedants." Academics in this reading take poetry both too seriously and not seriously enough. When Ammons tells us that he "believe[s] in fun," he is distinguishing his attitude from those who see no "fun" at all in poetry, who think that only a serious scholarly discussion of influence or form can properly deal with the virtues of the medium. And he contrasts his "fun" to "'superior amusement,'" which he finds "a little shitty," a little too sophisticated and refined for the pleasures that a poem provides. In his double-edged way, he even connects his "fun" to the fundamental premises of our culture, stating: "fun is nice: it's what / our society is built on: fun in the enterprise: I believe in it." Instead of performing the functions of a high priest with sacred relics, Ammons would prefer to play the role of one who enjoys the fun a poem offers, claiming that fun in the enterprise is that upon which our society bases itself, the combination of work with enjoyment that is presumably the ideal of all people.

Ammons' attitude toward the power of poetry, however, is not only contrasted to the scholarly display of erudition that buries a poem in footnotes; it also distinguishes itself from the skeptical visions of the value of poetry as well, as we see when he tells us that he has "no faith in the scoffers," those who deny the true power of poetry because it isn't rational and cannot be definitively located. In Ammons' mind, these "scoffers" "are party-poopers who are / afraid they ought to believe in history or logical positivism and / don't have any real desire to do so." Because such scoffers are intellectually convinced that all processes ought to be rational and capable of determination, because they think they *should* believe in history, or logical positivism, or any other framework that provides clear explanations for things, they believe that they ought to submit poems to the same procrustean bed these structures impose on everything else. For Ammons, these types "are scarcely worth a / haircut" because they hypocritically speak of the necessities of history or logic when in fact they have no "real desire" to believe in such things. History and logical positivism are simply excuses for avoiding the true force of the poem, hardly means through which that power is explained and articulated.

Ammons' refutation of the scoffers and those who take everything too seriously is both to poke fun at them by calling them "party-poopers," and to assert in opposition to their views a simple statement about the nature of life and poetry: "organisms, I can tell you, build up under the thrust to / joy and nothing else can lift them out of the miry circumstance." The traditional Western view is that only some "rational" form like history of logical positivism is capable of lifting human beings out of the "miry circumstance" in which their lives are generally sunk—and only these structures are thereby capable of making the human race better than it is. Ammons' logic suggests otherwise. Organisms as a whole can only lift themselves out of the miry circumstance by building "up under the thrust to / joy," the ecstatic transformation of their lives that puts them in tune with the larger patterns of which they are a part. And inasmuch as we too are organisms, this is the only way for us to lift ourselves out of the miry circumstance of life. Reason won't do it; history won't; nor will any other elaborately conceived plan that is based on a denial of the basic fact that we too are organisms. If we accept that we are, then we too must be committed to the same basic thrust to joy, however much we might want to think that reason or history significantly differentiates us from other organisms.

As for poems, we are told that they are "pure joy, however divisionally they sway with grief." The value of poetry inheres in the fact that it is "pure joy," revealing to us that thrust that underlies our own commitment to the world and that establishes our understanding of the mechanisms of which we are a part. Even though poems also "divisionally . . . sway with grief"—as they must because they reflect the mortal state of organisms—the joy predominates, just as in Stevens' aesthetic the beauty of the world included both pain and evil. Ammons' vision is also based on living in the physical world, so he does not deny that pain and evil are a part of the miry circumstance of life, an unavoidable part. But the aesthetic appreciation of the one:many mechanism allows us to lift ourselves out of the pain and evil in order to see the larger patterns from which they derive. Poetry, then, is as

Stevens said, both "part of the res" and about it at the same time. It too functions like a living organism, but at the same time it also articulates for us the joy that is at the center of our being.

As a part of the world and a commentary upon it as well, poetry provides a dual reflection on the mechanisms of life. Poems are valuable because they are "verbal / symbols for these organizations" (49), and

> . . . they imprint upon the mind
>
> examples of integration in which the energy flows with maximum
>
> effect and economy between the high levels of oneness and the
>
> numerous subordinations and divisions of diversity. . . . (49)

Poetry is capable of generating joy because it is such a splendid example of "integration," because it both integrates and allows the "energy" of that integration to flow "with maximum / effect and economy between . . . oneness and . . . diversity." Not only are we capable of discerning the nature of relation through this poetic integration, we are also able to see the oneness of the pattern and the diversity inherent in it as well. The effect of such perception is joy—poetic, aesthetic understanding of the way the aesthetic mechanisms of the world work. And while other forms and experiences can provide us with the same integration, none can do it any better than poetry.

Inasmuch as Ammons' poetic treatise on the nature of the aesthetic is based within a physical world, and inasmuch as it presumably has to do also with the ethical, we must finally ask ourselves what such examples of integration have to do with the good, and at first Ammons seems willing only to offer up the traditional response about the "uselessness" of poetry. For him "it is simply / good to have the mind exposed to and reflected by such examples" (49), and that seems to be enough. The "good" of poetry needs no further justification than this, as it certainly doesn't have any immediate practical application. Presumably the examples of poetry make us more human in some way, but there is little that can be said about *how* they go about doing so. And Ammons is insistent on this point. Poetry

> . . . firms the mind, organizes its energy, and lets the controlled
>
> flows occur: that is simple good in itself: I can't stress that
>
> enough: it is not good for something else. . . . (49)

The "good" of poetry, then, derives from its ability to "firm" the mind, which in turn "organizes its energy, and lets the controlled / flows occur." In firming our minds, poetry provides a structure through which our mental energy can be organized, which in turn allows us to maintain the "controlled flows" through which we see the pattern and the energy of the world as a whole.

Poetry cannot give us the controlled flows themselves; it can only allow them to occur. What prompts them, how we arrive at them, and what we do with them are things beyond the control of poetry and our own conscious designs. But poetry can make it possible for such flows to come about, and it can help us appreciate the significance of them when they do occur. And insistently Ammons declares "that is simple good in itself." Poetry need do no more than that because this good is good in itself, requiring no additions to make it valuable and needing no other justification. This is Ammons' version of "poetry makes nothing happen," but it is much more powerful than the classic Modern statement of the value of poetry because it shows that poetry doesn't *have to* make anything happen to be highly significant and essential to our lives. Indeed, it does make something happen by firming the mind and allowing the controlled flows to occur; it simply avoids direct application to the world because its goal is an aesthetic rather than a practical one.

Ammons' description of the way that poetry makes nothing happen also allows him to take a turn that the Moderns avoided. He can stress that poetry is *not* "good for something else," but then, as he does immediately after this line, he can also assert: "although of course / it is good for infinite things else" (49,50). The Modernists found it debasing to poetry to imagine it as having a practical value; it was valuable precisely because it had nothing to do with everyday life. This, after all, was what allowed it to exist in its own discrete realm, and this in turn allowed the aesthetic to become an escape from the pain and evil of the world. Ammons agrees in part that poetry is a good in itself, but inasmuch as he doesn't separate the aesthetic from the rest of the world, he can also see the ways in which it is good for "infinite" things else. First and foremost, it is good for other things because it

> is the symbolical representation of the ideal organization, whether
>
> the cell, the body politic, the business, the religious
>
> group, the university, computer, or whatever. . . . (50)

Far from representing only its own order, a poem is capable of demonstrating the "ideal organization"; thus, its order reveals things about other orders as well, regardless of whether they are cellular in nature—reflections of the natural world—or political or other kinds of social order. To the extent that the poem allows us to discern the parameters of the ideal order, we should be able to measure the strengths and weaknesses of other orders, learning more about them in the process and distinguishing what can and should be altered in those orders over which we have some control. Poetry itself doesn't do this, of course; it only represents the ideal organization. What we can *do* with our understanding of that order, though, is most powerful indeed and has everything to do with our perception of the world around us. In this way alone the poem is an essential ethical instrument that is necessary if we are to evaluate the choices available to us.

The power of the ethical aspects of poetry prompts Ammons to wax a bit didactic, as he explains to us just why poems are taught in schools when poetry as a whole seems to be more or less inconsequential to our well being in the late twentieth century:

> . . . I used to wonder
>
> why, when they are so little met and understood, poems are taught
> in schools: they are taught because they are convenient examples
>
> of the supreme functioning of one and many in an organization of
> cooperation and subordination: young minds, if they are to "take
> their place in society" need to learn patience—that oneness is
>
> not useful when easily derived, that manyness is not truthful when
> thinly selective—assent, that the part can, while insisting on
> its own identity, contribute to the whole, that the whole can
>
> sustain and give meaning to the part: and when these things
> are beautifully—that is, well—done, pleasure is a bonus
> truth-functioning allows: that is why art is valuable. . . . (50)

The ethical value of poetry is displayed in two ways here. First, as "convenient examples of the supreme functioning of one and many in an organization of / cooperation and subordination," poems demonstrate the virtues of patience, the chief lesson of which is "that oneness is / not useful when easily derived, that manyness is not truthful when / thinly selective." This may seem a banal thing to learn, but as Ammons has already shown in the poem, it is precisely this kind of patience that is so hard for humans to learn and remember. Students are not the only ones who need to be reminded of this; we all forget it all too often. And to ascertain the proper mixture of oneness and manyness is to learn both how to evaluate properly and therefore how to choose. Without a sense of the dialectic between these two things, choice is always made from a "too thinly selective" representation of the context or else is corrupted by an all-too-easy sense of oneness that fails to represent the whole and the bits of reality. Quality of choice in any context is predicated upon a perpetually refined sense of the relationship between the one and the many, so poetry's ethical function helps us regularly to refine our sense of their relation and develop a more coherent sense of context.

A clearly developed sense of one:many, though, is in the end simply an expression of the good itself; it reflects that which is *well* done, and poetry serves to help us understand the larger question of the good as well, showing how it is developed out of the beautiful. As Ammons says, "when these things / are beautifully—that is, well—done, pleasure is a bonus / truth-functioning allows." Our sense of beauty derives from something that is well done, whether it be a natural pattern over which we have no control or a human construct designed to create pleasure, and our sense of the good in turn derives from the harmonies we see implicit in that which is beautiful. In contrast to the Moderns, though, Ammons points out that the "pleasure" of the beautiful is a "bonus / truth-functioning allows." The joy that we feel in the presence of the beautiful is not a goal in itself, something it became as the truth-value of art was called into question; the "truth-functioning" of poetry is still its primary purpose, its means of representing that which is good and beautiful, but it has not lost its ability to give pleasure—that is simply the bonus that occurs when we are in the presence of the truth, a consequence of our realization of the harmonies displayed before us.

Of course, the truth-functioning to which Ammons refers here is not the narrow or didactic kind that previous generations have found in art. It is rather the broadest of truth-functioning that is at stake, the unfolding of the one:many mechanism in all of its power and importance. The particular truths of localized contexts are not relevant to poetry, for its goal is not to instruct us about any specific way of life—it simply provides us with an understanding of the mechanisms through which we can make sense of life and arrive at the particular truths on our own. This is certainly not the kind of thing that a Samuel Johnson would have in mind in writing a poem like "The Vanity of Human Wishes," but Ammons' vision of the truth-value of poetry is more powerful because it becomes that which provides the particular truths of a poem like "Vanity" with their value. In restoring the truth-value of poetry, then, Ammons has given the aesthetic its rightful place once again, in contrast to those who insist that poetry not only makes nothing happen but also means nothing at all.

These "lessons" that poetry teaches have one other immediately obvious function:

> . . . in its [art's] changing, it pictures how
>
> organizations can change, incorporate innovation, deal with accidence
>
> and surprise, and maintain their purpose—increasing the means and
>
> assuring the probability of survival. . . (50)

In showing how organizations "change, incorporate innovation, deal with accidence / and surprise, and maintain their purpose," poetry demonstrates the ways in which all successful structures deal with the world of which they are a part. Change is inevitable, and so it is necessary to learn how to innovate, how to deal with the changes the environment presents the structure, and how to maintain the purpose of the structure in the process. Again, this knowledge has both local and universal applicability in countless ways every day, and in the largest sense it "increas[es] the means and / assur[es] the probability of survival." Only if we continually become more adept at mastering these processes will we be able to adapt sufficiently to maintain the survival of the human race, and we learn these things best via the presentation of the aesthetic in poetry and other art.

Having made the greatest of claims for poetry and demonstrated them admirably, Ammons is quick to pull back to the everyday, reminding us at the end of his poem that it has helped him pass the time in the midst of a raging snowstorm. He had to do something, and the poem proved to be a useful application, affording diversion, pleasure and knowledge. Although some might be offended by the idea that a poem can be written simply to "kill time" while waiting out a snowstorm, there is certainly no reason to think that great poems can't be made out of such circumstances, once we get beyond the foolish and all-too-serious notion of poets as orphic figures and poems as serious and solemn invocations of the mysteries of life. Poems are devoted to the mysteries of life, but those mysteries include the everyday as well as the largest of possibilities, and this too has been lost sight of too much in our rage to deify our poets.

"Essay on Poetics" is very much devoted to an aesthetic with specific ethical implications, then, but in order fully to appreciate how much this is so we need to say a bit more about the form of the poem, for it too is striking in its own way. To begin with, it is deliberately entitled an "Essay," suggesting Ammons' desire to merge the form of a longer poem with that of the prose form of an essay, complete with all that an essay entails. The casual style of the piece, combined with its colloquial language and its commitment to regular summations and articulations of specific relations among various points make it suitable as an essay and contribute to the overall flow of ideas throughout the poem. Ammons' goals are both lyrical and discursive, and he manages to bring both off because of his ability to mesh the oneness of the high, hard lyric with the manyness of the details and images that contribute both to the lyrical qualities of the piece and to its overall effect as an argument for a particular kind of aesthetic. There is a dialectic of forms in the poem as much as a dialectic of ideas or of the one:many mechanism, and it is the movement between forms, ideas and oneness:manyness that allows Ammons to show the kinds of patience and persistence that are required in order to achieve an understanding of the organization principle.

In turn, the movement of tone is equally great, as we encounter diction as diverse as "party-poopers" and "glistery astonishment." Prose pieces from texts on biological phenomena are included to "heave home" several points, among them the richness of diversity and oneness and the unity of poetic purpose that poems and some texts about the nature of living organisms share. And in the midst of it all stands Ammons' ubiquitous use of the colon, that permeable membrane of punctuation that requires a sentence to be read in both directions, suggesting precisely the kind of "sway" that Ammons must emphasize if he is to keep the reader's expectations for linear progress out of the way. Everything that sways forward implies a backward sway as well, and the colon is the best punctuation mark to represent this way of moving and thinking. Each of these devices thus contributes to the regular movement between forms, styles, ideas and levels of oneness and manyness and provide the poem with the suitable framework for establishing Ammons' aesthetic. And the mixture of lyrical statement and essayistic assertion combine to provide a point of coalescence that reinforces the notion that poems are simply good in themselves and yet good "for infinite things else" as well. The practical applications of the poem are endless, yet the specific details of it are coherent and fitting in their own, semi-autonomous context as well.

In contrast to Stevens' poetry, Ammons' is deliberately homey, reinforcing the fact that Ammons is comfortable within the physical world upon which his life and thought are based. Thus, his points are effectively conveyed precisely because he is willing to risk the everyday and banal in his work, a considerable risk when one considers the burden of grandeur the Moderns placed upon those poets who followed after them. The homeyness of Ammons' work allows him to show that it is possible to appreciate the aesthetic nature of the world and to live within it more or less comfortably, points that a writer like Stevens makes in a poem like "Esthétique du Mal," but points that are less convincing in his work simply because his rhetoric remains far removed from the physical world he presents to the reader. This is not to say that Ammons is a better poet than Stevens, but it does suggest that Stevens' vision is more appropriately articulated through Ammons' means than Stevens', and it also implies that the Whitmanian tradition is capable of manifesting itself in the late twentieth century in spite of all the events that seem to have undermined the grand optimism at the heart of so much of Whitman's work. Ammons is not as exuberant a poet as Whitman, nor is he as sanguine about the human future as Whitman was, but his work does convince us that there is still hope for the human species, just as it demonstrates that it is indeed possible to live in a physical world and to appreciate its aesthetic nature on a regular basis. And while this doesn't mean that Ammons' work "improves upon" Whitman's or Stevens', it does show that the aesthetic vision is increasingly the one toward which we must turn if we are to have any hope of living with ourselves and of living within the only world we have.

. . . . . .

If "Essay on Poetics" is devoted to a general exploration of the parameters of Ammons' aesthetic, the particular explorations of it are often more interesting in what they reveal about the implications of that aesthetic. A poem like "Corsons Inlet" is both more lyrical and more suggestive about what is at stake in learning to live in a physical world.

The poem centers on a walk that the poet has often taken—he knows the area well, and he returns on more or less the same course quite regularly. Indeed, the poem ends by emphasizing that yet another walk will be taken tomorrow. The walk the next day will be a "new walk," but it will also incorporate into it those things that have been observed before.

The three central characteristics of the walk are that it is circular, repetitive and pointless. The poet has no particular destination in mind, nor does he hope to accomplish anything per se during the walk. This "goallessness" allows the poet to be

> . . . released from forms,
>
> from the perpendiculars,
>
> straight lines, blocks, boxes, binds
>
> of thought[2]

that usually dominate the mind and provides him with another angle on the phenomena of the world, one that is based on "the hues, shadings, rises, flowing bends and blends / of sight." Because he doesn't have a destination or goal in mind, the poet doesn't have to impose a rigid structure on the environment around him. Instead, he can allow the forms that are already present to emerge into his consciousness. Thus, even though we are told again and again that precise goals and pure reason are the essence of accomplishment in this world, Ammons suggests that knowledge of the world can only present itself to us once we abandon those artificial ways of observing the things in our midst.

The circularity of the poem and the walk has the same effect. It announces that in a traditional way the poet has gone nowhere at all. He has not moved us into a new domain that transcends the earthly realm, nor has he allowed us to perceive a knowledge over and above the particular forms that are in our everyday lives. He has simply given back to us what we always already have: the world of emerging play and form as it appears to us on a daily basis. The value of our linear route through life has been denied, set aside, in favor of a path that returns upon itself to reveal to us where we have already been and where we shall be in the future.

In the same way, the repetition of the walk demonstrates the process through which we come to appreciate better the nuances of the world. Instead of always moving on to a new scene—the traditional mode of human exploration—the poet seeks to retrace his steps, going over ground he has already seen many times before. Because human perception is limited in what it sees at any given time, and because the world itself is constantly changing, one is capable of perceiving more if one heeds the changes in an area with which one is familiar. One forgoes the astounding effects to be discovered in a place that one has never encountered, but one gains a knowledge of the subtleties of the patterns of life that tend not to be visible without repeated encounters. As Ammons says, the walk is always new simply because both oneself and the area have changed, even if only slightly, so the repetition is always a repetition with a difference. And the difference is always that which allows one better to flesh out one's sense of reality, to gain a clearer sense of what Ammons called the "one:many mechanism" in "Essay on Poetics."

The nature of the walk in turn prompts a difference in orientation in the way the poet observes things. Instead of looking for specific things and directing his attention to those things he wants to find, he "allow[s]" himself "eddies of meaning: / yield[s] to a direction of significance." The scene itself prompts him to discover this or that "eddy" of meaning, and he simply "yield[s]" to whatever seems interesting in order to see where it takes him. Far from being the dominator here, the poet is willing to explore what comes to him in (seemingly) random fashion and remains unconcerned about the putative weakness of his method. He remains convinced that his "random" method is not random at all. He may indeed only take what comes to him rather than staking out an interest or a position in the first place, but the seemingly random display of nature always leads him into pattern, and the pattern always emerges in a methodical way, even if it is not as clear as the rationalist would like it to be. As Ammons puts it:

> by transitions the land falls from grassy dunes to creek
>
> to undercreek: but there are no lines, though
>
>   change in that transition is clear
>
>   as any sharpness: but "sharpness" spread out,
>
> allowed to occur over a wider range
>
> than mental lines can keep. . . . (44)

The patterns Ammons discerns are more difficult to track because their "sharpness" is "spread out," yet another oxymoronic way of expressing the tangible presence of pattern in a seemingly random world. The repetitions are necessary precisely because the sharpness is spread out, harder to see without the specific focus of "mental lines" to keep everything in place. But the patterns exist independently of the poet, and he must merely be attentive enough to them to return often enough to discern their overall parameters.

Once again, though, we are forced to consider the fact that the patterns Ammons wishes to point out are pointless. The simply *are,* and nothing of value can seemingly be developed from them. The rationalist can do nothing with them, and the entrepreneur is not interested in them at all, for they reveal the complexity of a world that always escapes the plans of localized commerce. They provide us with knowledge of the way the world works, but beyond that they seem to be of no redeeming social value. "So what?" one might say of Ammons' dexterous effort to reveal the patterns of late summer/early fall in a region of the country that most of us will never visit. Of what value is that? At best, it simply allows us to celebrate the marvels of the natural world. At worst, it distracts us from our more compelling interest in boxes and binds of thought, allowing our energy to seep away while we preoccupy ourselves with the meaninglessness of it all.

Ammons would argue, however, that these "meaningless patterns" are precisely the means to understanding our situation in the world, and thus the essential mechanisms whereby we come to discern the values upon which we operate and through which we choose. Unfortunately, these values are predicated not simply on pattern but on the implications of the patterns, and those are not always terribly appealing to humans, as Ammons' description of the scene before him reveals:

> the moon was full last night: today, low tide was low:
>
> black shoals of mussels exposed to the risk
>
> of air
>
> and, earlier, of sun,
>
> waved in and out with the waterline, waterline inexact,
>
> caught always in the event of change:
>
>   a young mottled gull stood free on the shoals
>
>   and ate
>
> to vomiting: another gull, squawking possession, cracked a crab,

> picked out the entrails, swallowed the soft-shelled legs, a ruddy
>
> turnstone running in to snatch leftover bits. . . . (44,5)

Here the patterns to be discerned are obvious: the pull of the moon moves the tides out, and because of the time of the year and the fact that the moon is full, the tides go out quite a way, exposing all the life on the periphery between water and sand to "risk." This in turn prompts the gulls to recognize a ready source of food, which they quickly devour to excess, not knowing when such a rich source of nutrients might appear again. And after the gulls have had their fill of mussels and crabs, "a ruddy / turnstone" comes in to eat up the leftovers. All of these events follow very precisely upon the slight shift in patterns that is connected to the seasons and the rhythms of the moon, and they are clearly discernible to anyone who wants to pay attention to them.

But these natural events are hardly pleasing to view, and they are all the more striking in that they occupy the space in the poem that would have been filled with a grand Romantic vision of the harmonies of nature in earlier poems. We see the harmonies here, but we also note that they are fairly grisly in their manifestations at times, and the blood and gore of life and death are not what we expected. Equally important, the poet is in the midst of these patterns and events; his perceptions of them are the perceptions of one who is affected by the same rhythms of life, albeit in a different way. Thus, even though the poet himself does not have to worry about being eaten by the gulls, the lessons of mortality—of the need for food and the violence that is necessary to obtain it—apply as much to him as they do to the "lesser" animals around which Ammons builds the scene. Nature has patterns that allow us to make sense of it, but the patterns themselves implicate us irretrievably in the life-and-death processes that nature finally is.

The summation of the processes the poem points to is straightforward and simple: "risk is full: every living thing in / siege: the demand is life, to keep life. . . ." "Risk is full" seems like such an obvious statement, yet it is the point we are so willing to miss in other presentations of the natural world, for risk, after all, implies all the things about being human we should prefer to ignore. Nevertheless, every living thing *is* in siege in an immediate and obvious way simply because it wants to keep the life it has. This is as true of humans as it is of mussels or gulls or anything else, though it is more easily masked in the human world where we do not as a rule witness the violence and death through which our own lives are sustained. To be alive means to be at risk, for the patterns of our world are indifferent to individuals and their circumstances. The sense of risk that ought to be inherent in any depiction of the aesthetic patterns of the world is that which gives them their joy, their awe and their fear. We are taken up by the patterns and see our place within them; we marvel at the large system of which we are an integral part; and we fear for our lives because we realize how small and unimportant a part of the pattern we really are. All of us are totally expendable. The patterns do not depend on us; we depend on them.

Once we see that the patterns of life are not innocent, and that we are implicated in them, we see that they are not neutral and meaningless at all. On the contrary, they become the means through which we bring order to our lives and the gauge of the values that emerge through the order we generate on the basis of them. At the same time, this means that the quality of our values is dependent upon our ability to discern the nuances of the patterns of which we are a part. Like Ammons, we need the repeated observation of and participation in these patterns in order to arrive at a sufficient understanding of them. Staying in one place is metaphorically preferable to moving on simply because the nuances are never available to us without a total immersion in the scene we are in the midst of.

The central values of Ammons' aesthetic, as we saw before, relate to the one:many mechanism. The dilemma inherent in these values is depicted in "Corsons Inlet" in the following way:

> pulsations of order
>
> in the bellies of minnows: orders swallowed,
>
> broken down, transferred through membranes
>
> to strengthen larger orders: but in the large view, no
>
> lines or changeless shapes: the working in and out, together
>
> and against, of millions of events: this,
>
> so that I make
>
> no form of
>
> formlessness. . . . (45,6)

To imagine one of the patterns of the world in terms of big fish eating smaller fish is to return to a fairly obvious biological cliché, but Ammons puts this cliché to new uses, for he is interested not simply in the way that larger orders depend on smaller orders and vice versa;

more importantly, he wants to show the careful way he must proceed in order to avoid violating the precision of his model. Because most of us tend to prefer either a totally determined or a totally random view of the world's events, we all too easily slip into ways of characterizing the worldly patterns that deny them their richness. Ammons asserts, however, that he can find "no / lines or changeless shapes" in the "large view." Nothing remains immutable and unchanging in this world, and there is no place of origin that would stop the movement of the patterns. So Ammons' order is "undercut" by the fact that it can never be perfectly discerned. As he says:

> . . . Overall is beyond me, is the sum of these events
>
> I cannot draw, the ledger I cannot keep, the accounting
>
> beyond the account. . . . (44)

Any final order the world might possess is surely beyond human ken, so Ammons simply turns away from such considerations altogether. He does what he can to arrive at an understanding of the orders of the world, but he is not seeking any final order.

But Ammons' poems are also devoted to allowing order to emerge, even if it seems to be an incomplete order to some. He carefully avoids making "form of / formlessness," for to see the world as an entirely random series of events is as absurd as imagining the final order that always remains beyond our grasp, assuming there is such a thing. Ammons is "liberated" on his walk; he does "yield" to that which surrounds him; but he does not give himself up to a random world and forego any responsibilities he has within it. He gives himself up to the world so that he can perceive the patterns that are in it, not to escape from pattern, and not to find the final pattern of all patterns. We exist between the possibilities we most often imagine, and the difficulty of living remains finding that between where our possibilities exist in their richest form. We cannot choose one or the other; we must live within their oscillation.

The difficulty of life from this perspective is simply that we tend to want to finalize our vision of things or else to forego questions of vision altogether. The liberating and constraining aspects of the aesthetic vision of the world are thus built into the fact that we shall never be able to achieve what we think we want to achieve, though we may be tempted to convince ourselves otherwise. Having perceived order and pattern, we may be inclined to imagine the end of our consideration of pattern, but we cannot do that if we are to remain truly living beings.

And this is the point that Ammons stresses most, ending his poem with yet another careful articulation of the circumscribed realm of virtuous choice:

> I see narrow orders, limited tightness, but will
>
> not run to that easy victory:
>
> still around the looser, wider forces work:
>
> I will try
>
> to fasten into order enlarging grasps of disorder, widening
>
> scope, but enjoying the freedom that
>
> Scope eludes my grasp, that there is no finality of vision,
>
> that I have perceived nothing completely,
>
> that tomorrow a new walk is a new walk. (46)

The "easy victory" of reducing the world to the narrow orders we perceive readily enough is clearly a temptation—otherwise the poet would not have to bring it up in the first place. Humans tend to desire closure of one sort of another, and the reduction of the world to the narrow orders we perceive is perhaps the easiest way of achieving a comforting sense of closure. The other way involves difficulty because it never ends. The poet must continually attempt "to fasten into order enlarging grasps of disorder" because the world will never be completely perceived. He cannot stop the arduous process of working with the world no matter how much he wishes to at times.

On the other hand, the poet's commitment to engaging the processes of the world means that he will continue to be able to "widen" his "scope," enlarging his understanding of the world and making his vision of things more accurate. Likewise, though he is hedged in by the fact that no final "Scope" will be available to him, Ammons sees this finally as a virtue rather than a limitation. He admits to "enjoying the freedom that / Scope eludes [his] grasp" rather than feeling acute disappointment at his inability to tie the world all together. The absence of a finality of vision allows him to appreciate the nuances of each walk he takes, making each walk a new one even if it is based on the same paths as yesterday's. The world thus remains an enriched place for us precisely because it cannot be locked into a finality of vision that would cover all its permutations. Our "walks" remain enjoyable and liberating because there is always something to see if we are willing to attend to it, and we are free because the world is always new in this way. We may be haunted by thoughts of an easy victory against the world at times, but we always end up the loser when we choose that easy victory. Ammons' road might be more difficult, particularly until we come to master its patterns, but it offers the richest perception of the world and provides us with greater enjoyment of life than would be possible in any other vision of things.

At the same time, the "terror" of our world is also something that needs to be discussed, and Ammons emphasizes this as well by making it such a central aspect of the poem. For most of us, it is hardly heartening to hear the poet tell us that there is "no arranged terror: no forcing of image, plan, / or thought," that "terror pervades but is not arranged." Since it is terror itself that we want to avoid, it generally matters little whether or not it is arranged or random terror. But the poet thinks that the distinction between arranged and random terror is important: because the terror isn't arranged—it couldn't be in a world where the natural patterns are always changing and where there is no finality to them—it isn't personal. We may well have to experience terror as an inevitable part of being alive, as a necessary aspect of being regularly at risk in the world—it is in one sense nothing more than the psychic residue in all of our actions that acknowledges the fact that immediate and total oblivion is always one of our possibilities—but we should be content to know that the world has nothing against us per se. Whatever we experience is simply the result of the endless play of events in the world, no more, no less. In addition, we know that terror is simply the physiological response to threat, to risk, to fear for one's life, and even if we should prefer not to have to face such things, life involves risk, which in turn involves terror. As with Stevens' "mal," we must simply learn how to accept this aspect of life and put it in its place so that it doesn't overwhelm us. Otherwise, we shall be running from the terror throughout life and shall miss the life we are trying to save.

There are, as always, compensations for seeing the world the way it is rather than blithely trying to hide from it, but in "Corsons Inlet" these aren't as obvious as they might be. The serenity of the poet's vision suggests the most important compensation: the poet lives fully because he exists within what is, accepts those things that cannot be changed and works within them. His fascination with the world is sufficient in itself, and the new things that he can see every day are enough to keep him interested and enchanted for a lifetime. This point of view is expressed frequently in other poems, "Gravelly Run," for example:

> I don't know somehow it seems sufficient
>
> to see and hear whatever coming and going is,
>
> losing the self to the victory
>
> of stones and trees,
>
> of bending sandpit lakes, crescent
>
> round groves of dwarf pine. . . . (11)

Although the "I don't know," the "somehow," and the "seems" provide a Stevensian kind of uncertainty in the background of the poem, still we can see that for the most part it *is* sufficient simply "to see and hear whatever coming and going is." We don't need larger frameworks for our lives to appreciate fully what the world is like, and observation and participation ought to be enough. While we may pull back from "losing the self to the victory / of stones and trees" because we like to remain in control, once we have given ourselves over to the natural world, it suffices perfectly and provides us with what we need. Our fierce possessiveness of self is better left behind for a greater appreciation of the way that self fits into the world of stones and trees. In giving it up, we free ourselves to observe the patterns around and within us, and so we haven't really given up the self so much as we have redefined its possibilities. It no longer has the control we wanted it to have, but it fits into the world more appropriately than we previously thought, and we can thus see how well integrated into the world we are.

At the same time, by the end of the poem it is clear that the natural world is not all that hospitable to humans, however much it is possible for us temporarily to immerse ourselves in it. If we learn to know the self

> . . . as it is known
>
> by galaxy and cedar cone,
>
> as if birth never found it
>
> and death could never end it, (11)

we also learn our total insignificance and the world's harsh indifference to our presence here. Unlike the Romantics who would find some religious whole to bring us more comfortably together with the world, Ammons can only conclude:

no use to make any philosophies here:
  I see no
god in the holly, hear no song from
the snowbroken weeds: Hegel is not the winter
yellow in the pines: the sunlight has never
heard of trees: surrendered self among
  unwelcoming forms: stranger,
hoist your burdens, get on down the road. (11)

This winter scene is a forbidding one, folded around with death and the cold of absolute zero, and no comfort is to be found. No philosophies will do, for nothing can make this scene more pleasant than it is. The holly may be green, but it portends no eternal return for humans, and the world as a whole lacks the intelligence we try to ascribe to it. After all "the sunlight has never / heard of trees" and shall never hear of them. Everything simply is as it is, and in this environment we aren't likely to find anything else. Strangers to this world and partially alienated from it, we can only recognize these facts, and then—like Whitman shouldering his duds—"hoist [our] burdens [and] get on down the road." We need this knowledge of the forbidding side of nature, but inasmuch as there is nothing we can do about it, we need to move on after we have recognized it.

To be in nature and yet not a part of it at the same time; to wish to be a full part of it and yet to be full of terror at its alien face; these too are things that we must confront on the way to our knowledge of the world, and Ammons has never turned his head from them. The Romantic illusions may be gone, but the need to understand our strange relationship to that which surrounds us is as powerful as ever, and only a poet who has seen again and again the subtleties of the world can make us recognize the necessity for living within the world at the same time that he demonstrates our difference from it. Ammons is such a poet, and he is capable of reminding us of those things we need to know if we are to overcome our self-pity and actively participate in those possibilities with which the world presents us.

. . . . . .

As with Whitman's and Stevens' work, we see that Ammons' poems are designed to do nothing more than present the world as the poet sees it, yet the poems also manifest a very clear ethical view of that world. Ammons makes no pretense of having any answers about life; again, that is not the poet's job. He simply walks around within the world and writes what he sees. But what he sees—and more importantly the *way* he sees it—demonstrates a view of life that necessitates a revision of the way we make choices. If the prevailing world view corresponded to the vision of Ammons, then his work would merely suffice to present to us the values we already share, and as such it would simply help to refine our ways of knowing, no mean feat in itself. But because his aesthetic view is so different from our ways of seeing things, it compels a radical reappraisal of the ways we construe the world, the ways we make choices, and the ways in which we seek to effect changes in our lives. Ammons' aesthetic shocks us out of our traditional ways of seeing the world even though in itself it is hardly new—it goes back through Whitman, and back from there in one form or another to a good many poets dating back to the pre-Socratics. It is shocking only because we have worked against such ideas for so long that they still seem to us to be totally original.

One way or the other, though, the poetry itself demands more than a linguistic appreciation. It is not enough to be interested in the ways in which Ammons makes words work, nor is it enough to see him as part of a larger tradition. If we are to see his poems for what they are, we must begin to appraise the ways in which they prompt us to revise our thinking about the world, and if they do that we must perforce begin to reconsider the ethical aspects of all poetry. Ammons has performed his job of work as well as he could; it is we who have failed properly to value what he has done, and until we do so, his poems, like the work of all other poets, will remain all too irrelevant to the way we live our lives and the way we construct the world that will emerge from the choices we make every day.

CONCLUSION: THE AESTHETIC OF WORLDLY HOPES

When one begins to look for the ethical components in the poetry one reads, two things become immediately obvious. First, all poetry is seen as inherently ethical, and second, one finds that the proper language for speaking about the ethical aspects of poetry is hard to find. In the first case, it is too easy to assume that one finds the ethical in poems simply because one chooses to look for it there. After all, we well know that any lens through which one investigates a subject matter generates its own presuppositions and helps one to find exactly what one is looking for. So it is certainly true that "anything is ethical if you say it is," but there is much more to the problem than that. We have come to recognize, for example, that words themselves are markers of ethical choices, and we tend to make use of this notion all the time in "non-literary" domains. Orwell's famous "Politics and the English Language" demonstrates over and over again the political issues involved in choosing one's words, but underlying the ideological choices is clearly an ethical notion of how to behave in the world. We regularly attack politicians and bureaucrats for the way they "misuse" language, again implying that there are "right" ways and "wrong" ways to put words to use, as there surely are. But when it comes to poetry, we tend to back away from our awareness of the ethics of language. We might find studies on how this poet's abstract language removes him from the concrete world, or how that poet's concrete language removes him from larger social concerns; we might find yet another in an endless series of studies on the ways in which language fails to represent reality; and we might even find the occasional text that is devoted to the explication of what used to be called the poet's world view. But in none of these cases is the ethical aspect of the work discussed with any seriousness at all, and it is long past the time when we should begin to ask ourselves why this is so.

As I suggested early on, there are good reasons why we have shied away from serious discussions of the ethical aspects of literature. To begin with, we sought to keep literature from being misused, and ethical discussions of it all too easily lead to abuse. Most ethical considerations of texts quickly move in one of two ways, both of which are in the end really the same. The writer either uses the texts as a reinforcement for his own beliefs, and thus values texts themselves solely in terms of the way they correspond to or deviate from his own views of things. Or the writer takes a specific political perspective and applies its principles to texts in the same way, sorting out the "good" and the "bad" texts in terms of those which reinforce the political viewpoint or call it into question. For the most part there is no difference between these two approaches—one simply makes obvious its agenda, the other relies upon our tacit understanding of a more traditional agenda that is taken for granted by the average reader. In both cases, the text is sacrificed to the agenda. It does not expand the agenda or call it into question; it doesn't prompt a revision of it or even a hypothetical abandonment of it. It either backs it up, or the work at hand is considered inferior. We have been right to be wary of such writing, for it does fail to take literature seriously as literature, if such a thing can be accomplished. But we have been wrong to abandon the field altogether simply because an ethical consideration of texts engenders such hypothetical problems.

If we concede that any ethical consideration of texts that begins with an agenda is problematic, though, and if we also concede that we all approach literature in a way that reinforces our own attitudes toward it and ourselves, how are we possibly going to get away from the inherent difficulties in discussing the ethics of texts? There is no doubt, for example, that I have chosen to speak about Whitman's, Stevens' and Ammons' poems as I have because what I see in their work corresponds in many respects to what I believe truly is, and therefore I allow to emerge that which brings to the surface things of importance to me. Isn't that the same thing as having an agenda? The ready answer is that yes of course it is. The only question is whether there is a difference in the *kind* of agenda underlying my ethical consideration of these texts that prevents it from being nothing more than yet another political position in search of supporters. And naturally enough I would argue that there is a crucial difference. I have an agenda, if you will, and I seek to promulgate it as vigorously as I can, but at the same time I don't seek to tell people what to do with their lives or even how to look at poetry per se. I do believe that the ethical aspects of literature need to be confronted, but I readily acknowledge that there are many ways of doing this. And while I am arguing for a particular kind of world view, I at least like to think that the view itself succeeds or fails in terms of its viability. Either it is finally patently obvious that the world is the way poets like Whitman, Stevens and Ammons say it is, or no assent is forthcoming. And even if such assent appears, it does not lead to a series of "rules for life" that one must employ. Each of the poets I have discussed has deliberately avoided "telling people how to live." They are, after all, writing poetry, and it is not the poet's job to tell others how to live. They show as best they can the way the world is, and if one comes to agree with their view, then it is the responsibility of the reader to work out for himself the ways in which the view applies to his life, how it prompts changes in the way he does things, and so forth. No poet can provide those kinds of answers for a reader, and few poets seriously attempt that kind of thing. And neither do I. As with the poets, I promulgate a world view, but what the reader chooses to do with it is his business.

The problem, of course, is that writers with more obviously political agendas at times put forth the same arguments, and yet we see immediately that they have larger designs on us. And in the end the problem lies in our ability (or inability) to know anything of the world about us. Those who would most readily turn any approach into an agenda with the same flaws as the most blatantly political approach to texts would simply argue that inasmuch as we can never know the world outside of our linguistic presentations of it, all agendas are the same. They all rely on a belief that the agenda corresponds most clearly to "reality," and they all believe that their perception of that reality guarantees the viability of their vision and justifies whatever admonitions they make on the basis of it. Inasmuch as my own view depends on a belief that we can at least know some things about the world we live in with a fair degree of assurance, it assumes that I personally have knowledge of those grounding circumstances, and that knowledge in turn justifies whatever I choose to say. There is no argumentative means to overcome this problem, so I shall not attempt to provide any.

In the case of the ethical perspective I am arguing for, however, I would assert that there are two things that suggest there is indeed a difference between my approach and the more obviously political ones. The first is what could be called the "vagueness" factor. As with the poets, my work tells no one how to live. In that sense it seems all too nebulous. It offers a world view but promises no commandments for living, no goals to pursue, no clear choices to make. It is not designed to do that because that is not my business any more than it is the poet's. In my view, naturally, this is not "vagueness" at all but careful precision. It is seen as vague because people are accustomed to being given this specific kind of ethical information and either expect it or loathe it when they see it. Those who expect to find it are disappointed in such texts as mine for the same reason they are disappointed in poetry: it doesn't tell them how to live. Those who don't want to find it but are put off by the obvious ethical commitment of the text complain about "hidden agendas" that are all too vaguely described. In my view there is no hidden agenda.

The complement to this so-called vagueness is that I myself can readily imagine the viewpoint I have articulated as taking on a "reactionary" *or* a "progressive" cast. In the political parlance of the day, I can imagine a conservative position emanating from my world view just as easily as I can imagine a liberal position evolving from it. People tend to be either liberal or conservative, and their own proclivities would change the way my aesthetic vision of things manifested itself in their own lives. Of course, this too could be seen as a serious problem in my view. If one can imagine either reactionary or progressive applications of it, it must be hopelessly muddled. This would be simply another variation of excluded middles and the law of non-contradiction. If my theory truly had any value, by definition it could only be applied in one way, or so the notion goes. I would argue, however, that it is precisely *because* my view doesn't dictate such things that it is both ethical and yet radically different from those perspectives that deliberately impose a specific agenda on those who believe in it. If I have that kind of agenda in mind, then I am clearly failing in my task, for I have not foreclosed the possibility that my theory could manifest itself in patently "conservative" ways when I myself have basically "liberal" leanings. The point is that from my perspective this lack of specificity about such matters demonstrates that my viewpoint is indeed an agenda, but that it also differs in kind in important ways from those agendas that have such specific designs on people.

I shall return to this problem in a moment, but for now I want to deal with the other crucial reason why ethical considerations of texts have been abandoned, and it has to do with our desire to preserve literature from the incursions of the "external" world. We want to keep literature pure precisely because it can be put to use in so many ways and because when it is put to use in these ways it ceases to be considered literature. While there is no reason why literature shouldn't be put to other uses, it ought at the same time also to be treated as literature. Whether or not there is something specifically "literary" about such texts that differentiates them from other forms of writing is a question that has bedeviled writers for some time now, and it is obviously related to the degree to which literature as literature is different from the uses to which it can be put. The language of literature finally doesn't bear any characteristics that exclusively pertain to it, so there is no reason to think that its literariness inheres in this. In the end about the only characteristic that does seem for the most part to pertain solely to literature is the one emphasized over and over again in this century: in poetry, fiction, drama and the like there is "no road through to action." These forms are not designed to provide the specificity of response that we are accustomed to in journalism or other kinds of writing, and their goals are thus usually considerably different.

But if there is no road through to action in literature, it is also true that any literary text has within it any number of roads through to action. That is why it is put to so many different uses, and it is also why many critics want to confine it within its own structure so that it is not contaminated by other disciplines. And because critics have rightly been wary of the uses to which literature has been put, the ethical questions of texts have been stripped away along with all the other possible uses. For the most part we have been left with texts that are *only* literary, just as we have been left with the assumption that aesthetics itself is a discipline that is cut off from the others.

As Whitman and the other poets have shown, though, an aesthetic is irretrievably connected to an ethic, even when that ethic is one of containment and purity. The only difference here is that poets like Whitman and Ammons have an aesthetic in which literature is not contained, in which its importance spreads to every aspect of our world. What we need to develop, then, is a criticism that addresses these ethical aspects without turning literature into another discipline altogether. We must talk about these things, but we must also avoid turning literature into a series of prescriptions for a way of life rather than something that has nothing much to do with the pragmatic aspects of existence, at least in an immediate way. If we fail to do that, we shall continue to ignore the aesthetic that has been emerging for over 100 years now.

Certainly one of the reasons why poetry is so little read in the United States these days is that it is perceived to have nothing of ethical value inherent in it. We have tended to focus on the obscurity and difficulty of poetry and other forms of literature as the reasons for the lack of readership, and there is doubtless some truth to that. But equally important is the fact that we have—for other reasons—deliberately tried to strip it of those things that many people originally expected from it. If literature doesn't have a meaning in the old-fashioned didactic sense, we have argued, then it doesn't have meaning at all. In emphasizing an aesthetic that is devoid of ethical concerns, we have proffered a view of literature as writing whose only point is the writing. Little wonder, then, that those who expect more from literature than pleasing phrases and interesting rhymes have lost interest in "serious" literature. We have *taught* them to lose interest by the way we have talked about it. We need instead to address literature as a whole, rather than a partial, thing; we must discuss it as a medium that is crucially involved in the ethics of the world rather than above the human fray. If we can do that without resorting to the older forms of didacticism, then we shall perhaps do something to reintegrate literature into the larger cultural processes.

The training of critics is also problematic in this context, though, for we are, after all, taught to be squeamish about ethical matters. "Cultural relativism" has been central to the university's way of doing business for some time now, and we have thus created two generations of critics who for the most part feel that they have no business taking a position on anything more important than the way to read a text. This would be perfectly legitimate if the ethical implications of the way one reads texts were also central to the critic's discussion, but they are not. We simply feel that we have no right staking out the ethical claims for a text, both because we might simply be making use of the text for our own purposes and because we don't want to offend anybody who might have a different view. We are all entitled to our particular vision of the world, so the theory goes, and it is wrong to call another's view into question. But this kind of perspective avoids the very purpose of criticism, which is to make choices and value some things over others. We do this only occasionally, and when we do, we confine our valuation to the quality of the text in purely literary terms. So our pedagogy further erodes the status of the very literature we are seeking to preserve and uphold.

If we choose to include within our discussions of the literary the ways in which literature is an ethical act, though, how can we avoid the kinds of discourse that are most amenable to agendas of particular kinds and the exertion of power for its own sake? In the broadest sense, we cannot avoid agendas, but then we are not avoiding them at present either. If every written document is an assertion of a particular view of the world, then inevitably it carries with it a spoken or unspoken agenda, and there is simply no way of getting around this fact. The only question in this case is whether the writer is aware of the implications of his perspective and makes them clear to the reader, or whether he is ignorant of the implications and/or prefers to hide them as much as possible.

In the narrower sense, however, it is possible to limit the ways in which we seek to espouse our own views through another text. It is a difficult task, for our views come with us in everything we do, but we can make use of the New Critical emphasis on the particulars of the text and simply do what we can to confine our remarks to what is actually in front of us. Granted, no text lives in isolation, and no text is an object. Nevertheless, the process of the text is fairly self-contained, and there is no reason why it can't provide a useful limit to our enthusiasm for our own ideas. Beyond that, we can only keep in mind the ways in which our agendas seriously undermine the quality of our commentaries by overwhelming the text at hand with things that have little to do with it. If we can be guided by those very straightforward "rules," then the ethical can indeed be discussed without leading to a totally politicized kind of criticism. The gain in such criticism would simply be that we would once again be articulating the larger parameters in which and through which literature works, and this would allow us more fully to express the useful uselessness of those texts whose value means so much to us.

Without a new commitment to the ethical nature of literary texts, we shall continue to contribute to the increasing sterility of literature. We will continue to talk about it as history, as politics and as "pure" writing, but we shall have lost the richer context out of which literature comes, and in so doing we shall cause it to have less rather than more value in the world. We may continue our old ways, as Ammons suggests, "in order to prevent the commission of / larger error" because "safe error is a pedantic preference well-known," but we ought to have the courage to face the text in all of its richness rather than turn away from it. If we cannot do that, then we ourselves are conceding the weakness of literature and helping it to become weaker. But we can also present the aesthetic of "worldly hopes" that writers like Whitman, Stevens and Ammons have given us and allow it to manifest its full range of possibilities, and we owe it both to ourselves and to the work we love most to do just that.

NOTES

Introduction

1. Czeslaw Milosz, "Not This Way," *Bells in Winter*, trans. Czeslaw Milosz and Lillian Vallee (New York: Ecco Press, 1978), p. 9.

2. Wallace Stevens, "Esthétique du Mal," *The Collected Poems of Wallace Stevens* (New York: Alfred A. Knopf, 1954), p. 325.

3. Stevens, "Description Without Place," *Collected Poems*, p. 345.

4. Friedrich Nietzsche, *One the Genealogy of Morals*, trans. Walter Kaufmann (New York: Random House, 1967), p. 219.

5. Jacques Derrida, "Structure, Sign and Play in the Discourse of the Human Sciences," in *The Structuralist Controversy*, eds. Richard Macksey and Eugenio Donato (Baltimore: Johns Hopkins University Press, 1972), p. 265.

Chapter One

1. Walt Whitman, *Leaves of Grass*, eds. Sculley Bradley and Harold W. Blodgett (New York: W. W. Norton & Company, 1973), p. 29. Subsequent quotations from "Song of Myself" are from this edition and will be noted with line numbers parenthetically in the text.

Chapter Two

1. Wallace Stevens, *The Collected Poems of Wallace Stevens* (New York: Alfred A. Knopf 1954), p. 128. Subsequent quotations from this poem are from this edition and will be cited parenthetically with stanza numbers in the text.

2. Stevens, "Of Modern Poetry," *Collected Poems*, p. 239.

3. Stevens, "Esthétique du Mal," *Collected Poems*, p. 313. Subsequent quotations from this poem are noted parenthetically in the text with stanza numbers.

Chapter Three

1. A. R. Ammons, *Selected Longer Poems* (New York: Norton, 1980), p. 30. Subsequent quotations from this poem are from this edition and are noted parenthetically with page numbers in the text.

2. A. R. Ammons, *The Selected Poems: 1951–1977* (New York: Norton, 1977), p. 43. Subsequent quotations from this poem are from this edition and are noted parenthetically with page numbers in the text.